NINE MODE

NINE
MODERN
POETS

An Anthology

SELECTED AND EDITED BY

E. L. Black

*Principal, Middleton St George
College of Education,
near Darlington*

M

Macmillan Education

First edition 1966
Reprinted 1968, 1969, 1970 (twice), 1973, 1974 (twice),
1975, 1976, 1977, 1978, 1981 (twice), 1982, 1985, 1986

Published by
MACMILLAN EDUCATION LTD
Houndmills, Basingstoke, Hampshire RG21 2XS
and London
Companies and representatives
throughout the world

Printed in Hong Kong

ISBN 0–333–01464–2

CONTENTS

R. S. THOMAS   *page* 115

DYLAN THOMAS   131

PHILIP LARKIN   149

PREFACE

WHEN, in 1912, Yeats read Sir Herbert Grierson's new edition of Donne, Yeats wrote to the editor: *I . . . find that I can at last understand Donne. Your notes tell me exactly what I want to know. Poems that I could not understand or could but vaguely understand are now clear.* It must be the aim of an editor to achieve a similar ideal, to tell the reader those facts about a poet and his works that will aid appreciation and will remove any barrier that the passage of time or the youthfulness of the reader has erected.

The nine poets here need different degrees of assistance from an editor. A kind of geometrical progression applies to the study of Yeats: gaining a little more knowledge about his life, his friends, and the significance that he consistently attached to his favourite symbols, suddenly deepens your response to his poetry. Eliot is a unique figure in literature, a poet whose major works are sometimes almost meaningless without notes. Auden was so topical in the 1930's that a modern editor of his early poems has two difficult tasks — to judge which are *not for an age but for all time*, and to assess how much help the contemporary reader needs in understanding pre-war politics. When he moves on to Auden's later poems he has the problem of revealing the consistent development hidden below the surface. In exploring Dylan Thomas's poetry an editor often has to search for the hard bed of argument beneath the torrent of words; in considering the imagery of Ted Hughes he must stress its accuracy as well as its violence. Owen, Betjeman, R. S. Thomas and Larkin hardly need an editor, but the reader needs encouragement to find powerful and sincere emotions in their poetry.

The editor must do more than explain the meaning of a

poem: he must help the reader to respond to its emotion. If not, the editor will merely have taught the reader to regard poetry as Byron regarded Horace's odes:

> *Then farewell Horace, whom I hated so*
> *Not for your faults, but mine. It is a curse*
> *To understand, not feel, your lyric flow,*
> *To comprehend, but never love, your verse.*

Unless the editor can help the reader to achieve a better attitude than this, the reader will say (justly) about his notes what Pope said (unjustly) about Theobald's notes to Shakespeare:

> *The things, we know, are neither rich nor rare,*
> *But wonder how the devil they got there.*

ACKNOWLEDGEMENTS

THE editor and publishers would like to thank the following, who have kindly given permission for the use of copyright material: Messrs. J. M. Dent & Sons Ltd., for the poems from *Collected Poems*, by Dylan Thomas; Messrs. Faber & Faber Ltd., for the poems from *Collected Shorter Poems*, *Nones* and *The Shield of Achilles*, by W. H. Auden, 'Sweeney Among the Nightingales' and 'Whispers of Immortality', from *Collected Poems* and 'The Dry Salvages', Part I, from *Four Quartets*, by T. S. Eliot, five poems from *Lupercal* and three poems from *The Hawk in the Rain*, by Ted Hughes, and 'The Whitsun Weddings' and 'An Arundel Tomb', from *The Whitsun Weddings*, by Philip Larkin; Messrs. Rupert Hart-Davis Ltd., for the poems by R. S. Thomas; the Marvell Press, for eight poems from *The Less Deceived*, by Philip Larkin; Messrs. John Murray (Publishers) Ltd., for the poems from *Collected Poems*, by John Betjeman; Mr. Harold Owen and Messrs. Chatto & Windus Ltd., for the poems from *Collected Poems*, by Wilfred Owen, and Mrs. Yeats, for the poems from *The Collected Poems of W. B. Yeats*.

W. B. YEATS

WILLIAM BUTLER YEATS (1865–1939) was born in Dublin and was an active patriot who longed for an independent Ireland. His father and brother were painters, so it is not surprising that he derived some of the distinctive imagery of his poems from paintings and mosaics. His mother, Susan Pollexfen, came from Sligo in western Ireland; his many references to this locality show the intensity of his feeling for her family, and for the market town with its busy harbour, its river full of salmon, and its views of the nearby mountains such as Ben Bulben.

After unhappy years at a private school in London and some training as an art student in Ireland, he began to write poetry in a style inspired by the Romantics. The best known of his early poems is 'The Lake Isle of Innisfree', which has always had a popular appeal because homesickness is so fundamental a human emotion. His early love poems are full of a pleasant indolent languor and romantic emotionalism, for Yeats has not yet succeeded in putting into words the full intensity of his emotional experience, and his early poems lack the rhythmic energy and strength of his later poetry.

Quite early in life he developed an intense interest in unusual religious beliefs. He once said, *I am very religious and, deprived by Huxley and Tyndall, whom I detested, of the simple-minded religion of my childhood, I had made a new religion, almost an infallible church of poetic tradition of stories, passed on from generation to generation by poets and painters with some help from philosophers and theologians.* He came to believe that any symbol that had been used by any religion had become part of every man's subconscious, and that he was therefore justified in using it as a symbol in his poetry.

In 1889 Maud Gonne, a very beautiful young woman who had given up aristocratic society in Dublin in order to work for the cause of Irish nationalism, visited him to tell him how much she admired his poetry; he found her beauty far greater than he ever expected to see in a living woman — *It belonged to famous pictures, to poetry, to some legendary past.* He repeatedly proposed marriage to her between 1889 and 1903, when he was terribly shocked to receive a telegram to say that she had married John MacBride. He was a national hero because he had fought with the Boers against the English but Yeats hated him as a vulgar demagogue. From 1889 to 1903 Yeats and Maud Gonne had worked together in a nationalist movement that was partly literary and partly political, though she was always more bitter towards the English than he was. For instance, on the day of Queen Victoria's Diamond Jubilee, she was so indignant at finding herself locked out of a cemetery where she had intended to decorate the graves of Irish political martyrs, that in the evening she provoked a riot. She inspired Yeats to write two nationalist plays, *The Countess Cathleen* (1892) and *Cathleen ni Houlihan* (1902); the legendary heroine of the first play is a projection of Maud Gonne, and the central character of the second play (a representation of Ireland) was played on the stage by her.

In the years immediately after 1899 Yeats was prominent in the management of the Abbey Theatre in Dublin. Lady Gregory, a widow who owned the mansion of Coole in western Ireland, devoted a lot of energy to the project, wrote plays for it herself, mothered the overworked Yeats, and made her home at Coole Park a salon where the leaders of Ireland's literary life could meet to argue or be left alone to write.

Between 1903 and 1914 Yeats wrote rather less poetry, but the American poet, Ezra Pound, admired in Yeats's poetry of this period *a new robustness* and *the tooth of satire*, qualities that we find in 'The Scholars' and a more serious political poem, 'To a Shade'. Today we see, more clearly than his contemporaries could, how his verse at this time was developing a sparer style, and a wider range of subject matter. His attitude to life was affected by a series of profound shocks. First there was the marriage of Maud Gonne. Secondly there was the hostile reception which the Irish gave to Synge's play *The Playboy of the Western World*. Yeats had found Synge in Paris in 1896 and had encouraged him to visit the Aran Islands and write the plays about Irish peasants for which he is still famous. In 1907 the Abbey Theatre, which seemed to Yeats an important part of Ireland's greatness, presented *The Playboy of the Western World*, a comedy in which the peasants of the Aran Islands welcome a young man who boasts he has killed his father. Yeats was bitterly angry when the predominantly Catholic audience objected to the play because they thought it made derogatory fun of Irish peasants, and because it used an immodest word, imagining the women of Ireland standing in their *shifts*. The Irish public behaved like ungrateful philistines; according to Yeats in *The Arrow*, forty men sat in the middle of the pit making a noise (some of them blowing tin trumpets) and five hundred policemen struggled in vain to keep order in the theatre and its neighbourhood. Yeats was angry that so fine a play should be received so badly, and his indignation was increased when Lady Gregory's nephew, Hugh Lane, offered to give his collection of French Impressionist paintings to the Dublin Art Gallery, but the Dublin public was too mean to build suitable rooms in which to exhibit them. Yeats's resentment at the ingratitude of his countrymen towards Synge and Lane helped to make his poetry less romantic and gave it a harsher grip of reality. But we must not explain away the improvements of his poetry as entirely due to his disappointments. It was a triumph of Yeats's character and technique that in his middle age he set himself to adapt to his own purposes the example of Synge (whose preface to his one thin volume of lyrics invited verse to be 'brutal') and the condensed thought and speech rhythms of Donne; from now on Yeats was able to write in a series of different styles about a wide range of topics.

On Easter Monday 1916 the Irish rose in rebellion against the English, and between 1916 and 1921 they fought the English in a guerrilla war of a type we have experienced in the 1950s in Cyprus. The English were stung into retaliation, and after the Armistice of 1918 a poorly disciplined force, nicknamed the Black and Tans, was provoked into committing ill-tempered atrocities. Even after 1921 rival Irish factions fought a civil war about whether to accept the Peace Treaty which gave independence to the Irish Free State but separated it from the six counties now known as Northern Ireland. Yeats was closely affected, though he never took part in the fighting, and the war became a major topic in his poetry. The shock that it gave him in revealing the more cruel and bigoted aspects of human nature altered his poetry as much as their participation in the 1914-18 War altered the poetry of Wilfred Owen and Siegfried Sassoon. He knew personally most of the men shot in 1916, and he remained emotionally involved in the 'terrible beauty' not only of their deaths but of the 'troubles' that followed. Near Lady Gregory's estate at Coole, which meant so much to him, roads were blocked, bridges blown up and rival combatants threatened to set fire to her house, while on her estate a woman tenant who was an innocent bystander was shot in cold blood by the Black and Tans. At Thoor Ballylee, the 'Tower' in which Yeats was living in 1922, the Republicans blew up the bridge one midnight and forbade him and his family to leave the house.

These dramatic events around him produced an equally dramatic change in his private life. Since MacBride had been shot, he proposed again to Maud Gonne, who had left her husband in 1905, but she rejected him again, and in October 1917, he married Miss Hyde-Lees, who had been a friend for some years. She brought maturity and serenity to both his poetry and his life. He pays her a deep-felt compliment in 'Prayer for my Daughter'.

> *Yet many, that have played the fool*
> *For Beauty's very self, has charm made wise,*
> *And many a poor man that has roved,*
> *Loved and thought himself beloved,*
> *From a glad kindness cannot take his eyes.*

After 1922 he did his best to serve the new Irish Free State as a Senator; but though he tried to influence the politics of the new state, he was critical of many of its actions. This led him to idealise the aristocracy who had often lost their big houses and great estates in the Troubles or had been forced to sell them through the pressure of death duties.

Soon after the publication in 1939 of his *Last Poems*, startlingly different in style from his previous poems, he died in France, but in 1948 the Irish Navy brought back his body to Galway in a gunboat so that it could be reburied in Sligo:

> *Under bare Ben Bulben's head*
> *In Drumcliff churchyard Yeats is laid.*

The poems of his maturity deal with the topics that interested him most — civil war, politics, friendship, love, the death of friends. They face with passionate honesty the problems of growing old. They are characterised by a fundamental sincerity, and by a poetic fusion of the fullest range of human sensations, emotions and ideas. He is able to do this because he can make his style rhetorical or severe, conversational or bardic, as the subject demands; and because his use of symbols gives emotional intensity to his poetry, provided that the reader approaches his occult ideas with that *willing suspension of disbelief that constitutes poetic faith.*

TO A SHADE

If you have revisited the town, thin Shade,
Whether to look upon your monument
(I wonder if the builder has been paid)
Or happier-thoughted when the day is spent
To drink of that salt breath out of the sea
When grey gulls flit about instead of men,
And the gaunt houses put on majesty:
Let those content you and be gone again;
For they are at their old tricks yet.

                         A man
Of your own passionate serving kind who had brought   10
In his full hands what, had they only known,
Had given their children's children loftier thought,
Sweeter emotion, working in their veins
Like gentle blood, has been driven from the place,
And insult heaped upon him for his pains,
And for his open-handedness, disgrace;
Your enemy, an old foul mouth, had set
The pack upon him.

                       Go, unquiet wanderer,
And gather the Glasnevin coverlet
About your head till the dust stops your ear,   20
The time for you to taste of that salt breath
And listen at the corners has not come:
You had enough of sorrow before death —
Away, away! You are safer in the tomb.

EASTER 1916

I HAVE met them at close of day
Coming with vivid faces
From counter or desk among grey
Eighteenth-century houses.
I have passed with a nod of the head
Or polite meaningless words,
Or have lingered awhile and said
Polite meaningless words,
And thought before I had done
Of a mocking tale or a gibe   10
To please a companion
Around the fire at the club,
Being certain that they and I
But lived where motley is worn:
All changed, changed utterly:
A terrible beauty is born.

That woman's days were spent
In ignorant good-will,
Her nights in argument
Until her voice grew shrill.   20
What voice more sweet than hers
When, young and beautiful,
She rode to harriers?
This man had kept a school
And rode our wingèd horse;
This other his helper and friend
Was coming into his force;
He might have won fame in the end,
So sensitive his nature seemed,
So daring and sweet his thought.   30
This other man I had dreamed
A drunken, vainglorious lout.
He had done most bitter wrong

B

To some who are near my heart,
Yet I number him in the song;
He, too, has resigned his part
In the casual comedy;
He, too, has been changed in his turn,
Transformed utterly:
A terrible beauty is born.   40

Hearts with one purpose alone
Through summer and winter seem
Enchanted to a stone
To trouble the living stream.
The horse that comes from the road,
The rider, the birds that range
From cloud to tumbling cloud,
Minute by minute they change;
A shadow of cloud on the stream
Changes minute by minute;   50
A horse-hoof slides on the brim,
And a horse plashes within it;
The long-legged moor-hens dive,
And hens to moor-cocks call;
Minute by minute they live:
The stone's in the midst of all.

Too long a sacrifice
Can make a stone of the heart.
O when may it suffice?
That is Heaven's part, our part   60
To murmur name upon name,
As a mother names her child
When sleep at last has come
On limbs that had run wild.
What is it but nightfall?
No, no, not night but death;
Was it needless death after all?
For England may keep faith
For all that is done and said.

We know their dream; enough   70
To know they dreamed and are dead;
And what if excess of love
Bewildered them till they died?
I write it out in a verse —
MacDonagh and MacBride
And Connolly and Pearse
Now and in time to be,
Wherever green is worn,
Are changed, changed utterly:
A terrible beauty is born.   80

IN MEMORY OF MAJOR ROBERT GREGORY

I

Now that we're almost settled in our house
I'll name the friends that cannot sup with us
Beside a fire of turf in th' ancient tower,
And having talked to some late hour
Climb up the narrow winding stair to bed:
Discoverers of forgotten truth
Or mere companions of my youth,
All, all are in my thoughts to-night being dead.

II

Always we'd have the new friend meet the old
And we are hurt if either friend seem cold,   10
And there is salt to lengthen out the smart
In the affections of our heart,
And quarrels are blown up upon that head;
But not a friend that I would bring
This night can set us quarrelling,
For all that come into my mind are dead.

III

Lionel Johnson comes the first to mind,
That loved his learning better than mankind,
Though courteous to the worst; much falling he
Brooded upon sanctity   20
Till all his Greek and Latin learning seemed
A long blast upon the horn that brought
A little nearer to his thought
A measureless consummation that he dreamed.

IV

And that enquiring man John Synge comes next,
That dying chose the living world for text
And never could have rested in the tomb
But that, long travelling, he had come
Towards nightfall upon certain set apart
In a most desolate stony place,   30
Towards nightfall upon a race
Passionate and simple like his heart.

V

And then I think of old George Pollexfen,
In muscular youth well known to Mayo men
For horsemanship at meets or at racecourses,
That could have shown how pure-bred horses
And solid men, for all their passion, live
But as the outrageous stars incline
By opposition, square and trine;
Having grown sluggish and contemplative.   40

VI

They were my close companions many a year,
A portion of my mind and life, as it were,
And now their breathless faces seem to look
Out of some old picture-book;

I am accustomed to their lack of breath,
But not that my dear friend's dear son,
Our Sidney and our perfect man,
Could share in that discourtesy of death.

VII

For all things the delighted eye now sees
Were loved by him: the old storm-broken trees   50
That cast their shadows upon road and bridge;
The tower set on the stream's edge;
The ford where drinking cattle make a stir
Nightly, and startled by that sound
The water-hen must change her ground;
He might have been your heartiest welcomer.

VIII

When with the Galway foxhounds he would ride
From Castle Taylor to the Roxborough side
Or Esserkelly plain, few kept his pace;
At Mooneen he had leaped a place   60
So perilous that half the astonished meet
Had shut their eyes; and where was it
He rode a race without a bit?
And yet his mind outran the horses' feet.

IX

We dreamed that a great painter had been born
To cold Clare rock and Galway rock and thorn,
To that stern colour and that delicate line
That are our secret discipline
Wherein the gazing heart doubles her might.
Soldier, scholar, horseman, he,   70
And yet he had the intensity
To have published all to be a world's delight.

X

What other could so well have counselled us
In all lovely intricacies of a house
As he that practised or that understood
All work in metal or in wood,
In moulded plaster or in carven stone?
Soldier, scholar, horseman, he,
And all he did done perfectly
As though he had but that one trade alone.   80

XI

Some burn damp faggots, others may consume
The entire combustible world in one small room
As though dried straw, and if we turn about
The bare chimney is gone black out
Because the work had finished in that flare.
Soldier, scholar, horseman, he,
As 'twere all life's epitome.
What made us dream that he could comb grey hair?

XII

I had thought, seeing how bitter is that wind
That shakes the shutter, to have brought to mind   90
All those that manhood tried, or childhood loved
Or boyish intellect approved,
With some appropriate commentary on each;
Until imagination brought
A fitter welcome; but a thought
Of that late death took all my heart for speech.

SAILING TO BYZANTIUM

I

THAT is no country for old men. The young
In one another's arms, birds in the trees
— Those dying generations — at their song,
The salmon-falls, the mackerel-crowded seas,
Fish, flesh, or fowl, commend all summer long
Whatever is begotten, born, and dies.
Caught in that sensual music all neglect
Monuments of unageing intellect.

II

An aged man is but a paltry thing,
A tattered coat upon a stick, unless   10
Soul clap its hands and sing, and louder sing
For every tatter in its mortal dress,
Nor is there singing school but studying
Monuments of its own magnificence;
And therefore I have sailed the seas and come
To the holy city of Byzantium.

III

O sages standing in God's holy fire
As in the gold mosaic of a wall,
Come from the holy fire, perne in a gyre,
And be the singing-masters of my soul.   20
Consume my heart away; sick with desire
And fastened to a dying animal
It knows not what it is; and gather me
Into the artifice of eternity.

IV

Once out of nature I shall never take
My bodily form from any natural thing,
But such a form as Grecian goldsmiths make
Of hammered gold and gold enamelling
To keep a drowsy Emperor awake;
Or set upon a golden bough to sing   30
To lords and ladies of Byzantium
Of what is past, or passing, or to come.

BYZANTIUM

THE unpurged images of day recede;
The Emperor's drunken soldiery are abed;
Night resonance recedes, night-walkers' song
After great cathedral gong;
A starlit or a moonlit dome disdains
All that man is,
All mere complexities,
The fury and the mire of human veins.

Before me floats an image, man or shade,
Shade more than man, more image than a shade;   10
For Hades' bobbin bound in mummy-cloth
May unwind the winding path;
A mouth that has no moisture and no breath
Breathless mouths may summon;
I hail the superhuman;
I call it death-in-life and life-in-death.

Miracle, bird or golden handiwork,
More miracle than bird or handiwork,
Planted on the star-lit golden bough,
Can like the cocks of Hades crow,
Or, by the moon embittered, scorn aloud   20
In glory of changeless metal

Common bird or petal
And all complexities of mire or blood.

At midnight on the Emperor's pavement flit
Flames that no faggot feeds, nor steel has lit,
Nor storm disturbs, flames begotten of flame,
Where blood-begotten spirits come
And all complexities of fury leave,
Dying into a dance,   30
An agony of trance,
An agony of flame that cannot singe a sleeve.

Astraddle on the dolphin's mire and blood,
Spirit after spirit! The smithies break the flood,
The golden smithies of the Emperor!
Marbles of the dancing floor
Break bitter furies of complexity,
Those images that yet
Fresh images beget,
That dolphin-torn, that gong-tormented sea.   40

THE TOWER

I

WHAT shall I do with this absurdity —
O heart, O troubled heart — this caricature,
Decrepit age that has been tied to me
As to a dog's tail?
                        Never had I more
Excited, passionate, fantastical
Imagination, nor an ear and eye
That more expected the impossible —
No, not in boyhood when with rod and fly,
Or the humbler worm, I climbed Ben Bulben's back
And had the livelong summer day to spend.   10
It seems that I must bid the Muse go pack,

Choose Plato and Plotinus for a friend
Until imagination, ear and eye,
Can be content with argument and deal
In abstract things; or be derided by
A sort of battered kettle at the heel.

II

I pace upon the battlements and stare
On the foundations of a house, or where
Tree, like a sooty finger, starts from the earth;
And send imagination forth   20
Under the day's declining beam, and call
Images and memories
From ruin or from ancient trees,
For I would ask a question of them all.

Beyond that ridge lived Mrs. French, and once
When every silver candlestick or sconce
Lit up the dark mahogany and the wine,
A serving-man, that could divine
That most respected lady's every wish,
Ran and with the garden shears   30
Clipped an insolent farmer's ears
And brought them in a little covered dish.

Some few remembered still when I was young
A peasant girl commended by a song,
Who'd lived somewhere upon that rocky place,
And praised the colour of her face,
And had the greater joy in praising her,
Remembering that, if walked she there,
Farmers jostled at the fair
So great a glory did the song confer.   40

And certain men, being maddened by those rhymes,
Or else by toasting her a score of times,
Rose from the table and declared it right

To test their fancy by their sight;
But they mistook the brightness of the moon
For the prosaic light of day —
Music had driven their wits astray —
And one was drowned in the great bog of Cloone.

Strange, but the man who made the song was blind;
Yet, now I have considered it, I find   50
That nothing strange; the tragedy began
With Homer that was a blind man,
And Helen has all living hearts betrayed.
O may the moon and sunlight seem
One inextricable beam,
For if I triumph I must make men mad.

And I myself created Hanrahan
And drove him drunk or sober through the dawn
From somewhere in the neighbouring cottages.
Caught by an old man's juggleries   60
He stumbled, tumbled, fumbled to and fro
And had but broken knees for hire
And horrible splendour of desire;
I thought it all out twenty years ago:

Good fellows shuffled cards in an old bawn;
And when that ancient ruffian's turn was on
He so bewitched the cards under his thumb
That all but the one card became
A pack of hounds and not a pack of cards,
And that he changed into a hare.   70
Hanrahan rose in frenzy there
And followed up those baying creatures towards —

O towards I have forgotten what — enough!
I must recall a man that neither love
Nor music nor an enemy's clipped ear
Could, he was so harried, cheer;
A figure that has grown so fabulous

There's not a neighbour left to say
When he finished his dog's day:
An ancient bankrupt master of this house.   80

Before that ruin came, for centuries,
Rough men-at-arms, cross-gartered to the knees
Or shod in iron, climbed the narrow stairs,
And certain men-at-arms there were
Whose images, in the Great Memory stored,
Come with loud cry and panting breast
To break upon a sleeper's rest
While their great wooden dice beat on the board.

As I would question all, come all who can;
Come old, necessitous, half-mounted man;   90
And bring beauty's blind rambling celebrant;
The red man the juggler sent
Through God-forsaken meadows; Mrs. French,
Gifted with so fine an ear;
The man drowned in a bog's mire,
When mocking Muses chose the country wench.

Did all old men and women, rich and poor,
Who trod upon these rocks or passed this door,
Whether in public or in secret rage
As I do now against old age?   100
But I have found an answer in those eyes
That are impatient to be gone;
Go therefore; but leave Hanrahan,
For I need all his mighty memories.

Old lecher with a love on every wind,
Bring up out of that deep considering mind
All that you have discovered in the grave,
For it is certain that you have
Reckoned up every unforeknown, unseeing
Plunge, lured by a softening eye,   110
Or by a touch or a sigh,
Into the labyrinth of another's being;

Does the imagination dwell the most
Upon a woman won or woman lost?
If on the lost, admit you turned aside
From a great labyrinth out of pride,
Cowardice, some silly over-subtle thought
Or anything called conscience once;
And that if memory recur, the sun's
Under eclipse and the day blotted out.   120

III

It is time that I wrote my will;
I choose upstanding men
That climb the streams until
The fountain leap, and at dawn
Drop their cast at the side
Of dripping stone; I declare
They shall inherit my pride,
The pride of people that were
Bound neither to Cause nor to State,
Neither to slaves that were spat on,   130
Nor to the tyrants that spat,
The people of Burke and of Grattan
That gave, though free to refuse —
Pride, like that of the morn,
When the headlong light is loose,
Or that of the fabulous horn,
Or that of the sudden shower
When all streams are dry,
Or that of the hour
When the swan must fix his eye   140
Upon a fading gleam,
Float out upon a long
Last reach of glittering stream
And there sing his last song.
And I declare my faith:
I mock Plotinus' thought
And cry in Plato's teeth,

Death and life were not
Till man made up the whole,
Made lock, stock and barrel   150
Out of his bitter soul,
Aye, sun and moon and star, all,
And further add to that
That, being dead, we rise,
Dream and so create
Translunar Paradise.
I have prepared my peace
With learned Italian things
And the proud stones of Greece,
Poet's imaginings   160
And memories of love,
Memories of the words of women,
All those things whereof
Man makes a superhuman
Mirror-resembling dream

As at the loophole there
The daws chatter and scream,
And drop twigs layer upon layer.
When they have mounted up,
The mother bird will rest   170
On their hollow top,
And so warm her wild nest.

I leave both faith and pride
To young upstanding men
Climbing the mountain-side,
That under bursting dawn
They may drop a fly;
Being of that metal made
Till it was broken by
This sedentary trade.   180

Now shall I make my soul,
Compelling it to study

In a learned school
Till the wreck of body,
Slow decay of blood,
Testy delirium
Or dull decrepitude,
Or what worse evil come —
The death of friends, or death
Of every brilliant eye   190
That made a catch in the breath —
Seem but the clouds of the sky
When the horizon fades;
Or a bird's sleepy cry
Among the deepening shades.

THE WILD SWANS AT COOLE

THE trees are in their autumn beauty,
The woodland paths are dry,
Under the October twilight the water
Mirrors a still sky;
Upon the brimming water among the stones
Are nine-and-fifty swans.

The nineteenth autumn has come upon me
Since I first made my count;
I saw, before I had well finished,
All suddenly mount   10
And scatter wheeling in great broken rings
Upon their clamorous wings.

I have looked upon those brilliant creatures,
And now my heart is sore.
All's changed since I, hearing at twilight,
The first time on this shore,
The bell-beat of their wings above my head,
Trod with a lighter tread.

Unwearied still, lover by lover,
They paddle in the cold
Companionable streams or climb the air;
Their hearts have not grown old;
Passion or conquest, wander where they will,
Attend upon them still.   20

But now they drift on the still water,
Mysterious, beautiful;
Among what rushes will they build,
By what lake's edge or pool
Delight men's eyes when I awake some day
To find they have flown away?   30

COOLE PARK, 1929

I MEDITATE upon a swallow's flight,
Upon an aged woman and her house,
A sycamore and lime-tree lost in night
Although that western cloud is luminous,
Great works constructed there in nature's spite
For scholars and for poets after us,
Thoughts long knitted into a single thought,
A dance-like glory that those walls begot.

There Hyde before he had beaten into prose
That noble blade the Muses buckled on,   10
There one that ruffled in a manly pose
For all his timid heart, there that slow man,
That meditative man, John Synge, and those
Impetuous men, Shawe-Taylor and Hugh Lane,
Found pride established in humility,
A scene well set and excellent company.

They came like swallows and like swallows went,
And yet a woman's powerful character

Could keep a swallow to its first intent;
And half a dozen in formation there, 20
That seemed to whirl upon a compass-point,
Found certainty upon the dreaming air,
The intellectual sweetness of those lines
That cut through time or cross it withershins.

Here, traveller, scholar, poet, take your stand
When all those rooms and passages are gone,
When nettles wave upon a shapeless mound
And saplings root among the broken stone,
And dedicate — eyes bent upon the ground,
Back turned upon the brightness of the sun 30
And all the sensuality of the shade —
A moment's memory to that laurelled head.

COOLE AND BALLYLEE, 1931

UNDER my window-ledge the waters race,
Otters below and moor-hens on the top,
Run for a mile undimmed in Heaven's face
Then darkening through 'dark' Raftery's 'cellar' drop,
Run underground, rise in a rocky place
In Coole demesne, and there to finish up
Spread to a lake and drop into a hole.
What's water but the generated soul?

Upon the border of that lake's a wood
Now all dry sticks under a wintry sun, 10
And in a copse of beeches there I stood,
For Nature's pulled her tragic buskin on
And all the rant's a mirror of my mood:
At sudden thunder of the mounting swan
I turned about and looked where branches break
The glittering reaches of the flooded lake.

Another emblem there! That stormy white
But seems a concentration of the sky;
And, like the soul, it sails into the sight
And in the morning's gone, no man knows why;   20
And is so lovely that it sets to right
What knowledge or its lack had set awry,
So arrogantly pure, a child might think
It can be murdered with a spot of ink.

Sound of a stick upon the floor, a sound
From somebody that toils from chair to chair;
Beloved books that famous hands have bound,
Old marble heads, old pictures everywhere;
Great rooms where travelled men and children found
Content or joy; a last inheritor   30
Where none has reigned that lacked a name and fame
Or out of folly into folly came.

A spot whereon the founders lived and died
Seemed once more dear than life; ancestral trees,
Or gardens rich in memory glorified
Marriages, alliances and families,
And every bride's ambition satisfied.
Where fashion or mere fantasy decrees
We shift about — all that great glory spent —
Like some poor Arab tribesman and his tent.   40

We were the last romantics — chose for theme
Traditional sanctity and loveliness;
Whatever's written in what poets name
The book of the people; whatever most can bless
The mind of man or elevate a rhyme;
But all is changed, that high horse riderless,
Though mounted in that saddle Homer rode
Where the swan drifts upon a darkening flood.

BEFORE THE WORLD WAS MADE

IF I make the lashes dark
And the eyes more bright
And the lips more scarlet,
Or ask if all be right
From mirror after mirror,
No vanity's displayed:
I'm looking for the face I had
Before the world was made.

What if I look upon a man
As though on my beloved,   10
And my blood be cold the while
And my heart unmoved?
Why should he think me cruel
Or that he is betrayed?
I'd have him love the thing that was
Before the world was made.

LAPIS LAZULI

I HAVE heard that hysterical women say
They are sick of the palette and fiddle-bow,
Of poets that are always gay,
For everybody knows or else should know
That if nothing drastic is done
Aeroplane and Zeppelin will come out,
Pitch like King Billy bomb-balls in
Until the town lie beaten flat.

All perform their tragic play,
There struts Hamlet, there is Lear,   10
That's Ophelia, that Cordelia;

Yet they, should the last scene be there,
The great stage curtain about to drop,
If worthy their prominent part in the play,
Do not break up their lines to weep.
They know that Hamlet and Lear are gay;
Gaiety transfiguring all that dread.
All men have aimed at, found and lost;
Black out; Heaven blazing into the head:
Tragedy wrought to its uttermost.   20
Though Hamlet rambles and Lear rages,
And all the drop-scenes drop at once
Upon a hundred thousand stages,
It cannot grow by an inch or an ounce.

On their own feet they came, or on shipboard,
Camel-back, horse-back, ass-back, mule-back,
Old civilisations put to the sword.
Then they and their wisdom went to rack:
No handiwork of Callimachus,
Who handled marble as if it were bronze,   30
Made draperies that seemed to rise
When sea-winds swept the corner, stands;
His long lamp-chimney, shaped like the stem
Of a slender palm, stood but a day;
All things fall and are built again,
And those that build them again are gay.

Two Chinamen, behind them a third,
Are carved in lapis lazuli,
Over them flies a long-legged bird,
A symbol of longevity;   40
The third, doubtless a serving-man,
Carries a musical instrument.

Every discoloration of the stone,
Every accidental crack or dent,
Seems a water-course or an avalanche,
Or lofty slope where it still snows

Though doubtless plum or cherry-branch
Sweetens the little half-way house
Those Chinamen climb towards, and I
Delight to imagine them seated there;   50
There, on the mountain and the sky,
On all the tragic scene they stare.
One asks for mournful melodies;
Accomplished fingers begin to play.
Their eyes mid many wrinkles, their eyes,
Their ancient, glittering eyes, are gay.

WHY SHOULD NOT OLD MEN BE MAD?

WHY should not old men be mad?
Some have known a likely lad
That had a sound fly-fisher's wrist
Turn to a drunken journalist;
A girl that knew all Dante once
Live to bear children to a dunce;
A Helen of social welfare dream,
Climb on a wagonette to scream.
Some think it a matter of course that chance
Should starve good men and bad advance,   10
That if their neighbours figured plain,
As though upon a lighted screen,
No single story would they find
Of an unbroken happy mind,
A finish worthy of the start.
Young men know nothing of this sort,
Observant old men know it well;
And when they know what old books tell,
And that no better can be had,
Know why an old man should be mad.   20

THE CIRCUS ANIMALS' DESERTION

I

I sought a theme and sought for it in vain,
I sought it daily for six weeks or so.
Maybe at last, being but a broken man,
I must be satisfied with my heart, although
Winter and summer till old age began
My circus animals were all on show,
Those stilted boys, that burnished chariot,
Lion and woman and the Lord knows what.

II

What can I but enumerate old themes?
First that sea-rider Oisin led by the nose   10
Through three enchanted islands, allegorical dreams,
Vain gaiety, vain battle, vain repose,
Themes of the embittered heart, or so it seems,
That might adorn old songs or courtly shows;
But what cared I that set him on to ride,
I, starved for the bosom of his faery bride?

And then a counter-truth filled out its play,
The *Countess Cathleen* was the name I gave it;
She, pity-crazed, had given her soul away,
But masterful Heaven had intervened to save it.   20
I thought my dear must her own soul destroy,
So did fanaticism and hate enslave it,
And this brought forth a dream and soon enough
This dream itself had all my thought and love.

And when the Fool and Blind Man stole the bread
Cuchulain fought the ungovernable sea;
Heart-mysteries there, and yet when all is said
It was the dream itself enchanted me:

Character isolated by a deed
To engross the present and dominate memory.   30
Players and painted stage took all my love,
And not those things that they were emblems of.

III

Those masterful images because complete
Grew in pure mind, but out of what began?
A mound of refuse or the sweepings of a street,
Old kettles, old bottles, and a broken can,
Old iron, old bones, old rags, that raving slut
Who keeps the till. Now that my ladder's gone,
I must lie down where all the ladders start,
In the foul rag-and-bone shop of the heart.   40

WILFRED OWEN

WILFRED OWEN was born at Oswestry in 1893. His father
was a railway official who moved in turn to Birkenhead,
Shrewsbury and Reading, where Owen attended a series
of technical schools. He was very fond of his mother, who
was keen on poetry and painting, and to whom he later
wrote long, literary letters.

As a boy he developed a very strong enthusiasm for the
poetry of Keats. This was to prove powerful and lasting;
the realism and horror with which he painted the landscape of the trenches of 1917–18 never prevented him from
seeing the kind of sensuous beauty in it that Keats would
have seen. Owen felt a sublimity in the intensity of the
horror, and poems such as 'Exposure' find a Keatsian
beauty in the flares and the flickering gunnery that
illuminated the cratered landscape as though they were
the fires of Hell. Not only did he feel a tremendous
admiration for Keats, but he imagined an actual affinity.
When on 17th September 1911, at the age of eighteen, he
saw a book in Keats's handwriting in the British Museum,
he wrote to tell his mother enthusiastically that: *His writing
is rather large and slopes like mine. . . . I seem to be strangely
familiar with it.*

Since his parents could not afford to send him to a
university, Owen went in 1911 to Dunsden, a village in
Oxfordshire, where he worked as a poorly paid lay
assistant to the vicar, who was supposed to educate him
for the Church; but visiting the wives of the rural unemployed made him so sorry for them that he lost most of
his faith in Christianity — until it came back to him in the
trenches in the form of an international faith that denied
all narrow patriotisms.

An illness in 1913 made him keen to avoid English
winters, so he taught English in Bordeaux until the

autumn of 1915 when he came home to enlist in the army. In January 1917 he went as an officer to join the Second Battalion of the Manchester Regiment on the Somme. On leaving England he had been excited at the prospect of joining *well-trained troops and genuine 'real-old' officers*, but at once he came face to face with the mud, misery and muddle of trench warfare. In a letter to his mother on 4th January 1917 he said: *Since I set foot on Calais quays I have not had dry feet. . . . After those two days* [at the base] *we were let down, gently, into the real thing, mud. It has penetrated now into that sanctuary, my sleeping bag. . . . We are never dry, and never 'off duty'. On all the officers' faces there is a harassed look that I have never seen before, and which in England will never be seen — out of jails. The men are just . . . expression-less lumps. . . . I censored hundreds of letters yesterday, and the hope of peace was in every one.*

Owen was learning very rapidly the cruel realities of war. Moreover, the Western Front had its special brand of horror; because there had been so little movement since 1914, the battles of 1917 and 1918 were fought among the collapsed trenches, ruined buildings and blasted trees left over from the previous battles. Owen was shocked and fascinated by the ghastliness of the scene; moreover, he was angered by the mismanagement that made the suffering of the troops even worse. Soon one of the coldest winters of this century added to the agony of the front-line troops and produced a landscape which he described in a letter on 19th January 1917: *No Man's Land under snow is like the face of the moon, chaotic, crater-ridden, uninhabitable, awful, the abode of madness. . . . The people of England needn't hope. They must agitate. But they are not yet agitated even.* Both his letters home and his poems stressed the universal ugli-ness of the scene, with the *unburiable bodies* of the dead becoming *the most execrable sights on earth.* Icy east winds whistled through the chaotic tangles of barbed wire. In the snow of No Man's Land men came simultaneously near to freezing to death and to dying of thirst, because they could not melt the ice as they lay with only a little

snow-covered ridge between them and the periscope of a
German sniper. The mud, when it was not frozen, was
an octopus of sucking clay. Even the bravest lost their
soldierly spirit when compelled to face all this for too long,
since —

> *Courage leaked, as sand*
> *From the best sand-bags after years of rain.*

In March 1917, and again two months later, Owen was
sent to a hospital in France suffering from neurasthenia;
from there he was transferred to Craiglockhart War
Hospital in Scotland, where he met the other great
English poet of the First World War — Siegfried Sassoon.
He was greatly encouraged by Sassoon's reception of his
poetry; he admired Sassoon's war poetry very much, and
admired, also, the moral stand Sassoon had taken, for
after being decorated for gallantry, the latter had come to
the conclusion that pacifism was the only possible answer
to the problem of modern war. Owen himself could never
quite decide whether it really was the lesser of two moral
evils to fight, when the alternative was to yield to tyranny.
His poetry rarely discusses this problem explicitly, but his
unresolved inner conflict adds intensity to all it says about
war.

In September 1918, he insisted on being sent back to the
front because he believed — rather unrealistically — that
there he would be in a stronger position to protest against
the war in the name of the front-line troops. On 4th
October 1918, after most of his company had been killed,
he and a young lance-corporal captured several German
machine-guns and scores of prisoners, for which he was
awarded the Military Cross. But on 4th November 1918,
he was killed while shepherding his company across the
Sambre Canal — for he looked on himself as an experienced veteran protecting the raw recruits in his care.
So the most promising English poet of this century was
killed a week before the end of the war.

Till 1917 he had been a young and inexperienced

versifier who occasionally hit upon an effective line such as
For earlier suns than ours have lent you gold, or *The sea is rising
. . . and the world is sand*. But the horror of trench warfare
added passion and realism to his poetry, and made his
genius mature with dramatic suddenness. He realised this
himself when he wrote in a letter: *Tennyson, it seems, was
always a great child. So should I have been but for Beaumont
Hamel* [the sector of the front where he had been fighting].
*Not before January 1917 did I write the only lines of mine that
carry the stamp of maturity.*

Many of the men who fought in the First World War
came to hate the English civilians sitting comfortably at
home, and ceased to hate the German soldiers shivering
with cold and fright a few yards away from them on the
other side of No Man's Land. They felt that the civilians
had caused the war by their stupidity, were making plenty
of money out of it, and could not imagine the horrors
endured by the soldiers. Sassoon makes this point
cuttingly: he imagines the typical dead soldier saying:

> *Two bleeding years I fought in France for Squire;
> I suffered anguish that he's never guessed.*

Owen occasionally felt like this; for instance, one letter
hopes that a U-boat will come right into Scarborough
Bay and kill *the stinking Leeds and Bradford war-
profiteers* reading magazines on the sands, and his poem
'Inspection' presents a satirical picture of a blood-stained
private being punished for appearing *dirty on parade*.
But it is a sure sign of Owen's greatness that he so rarely
imitates Sassoon; even when he is condemning those who
do not understand what war is really like, he does so more
positively than Sassoon, for he is not so much trying to
expose them as to convert them.

Owen's best poetry is greater than satire can ever be.
It is a noble appeal to all readers to feel *pity* for the men in
the front line in all wars, for unless we feel such pity we
shall never build a worthwhile world. In the Preface that

he scribbled for his as yet unpublished poems, Owen wrote:

My subject is War, and the pity of War.
The poetry is in the pity.

Yet these elegies are to this generation in no sense con-solatory. They may be to the next. All a poet can do today is warn. That is why the true Poets must be truthful.

The dominant moods of his poetry are an elegiac mourning of the dead and a passionate protest against the purposeless waste of their young lives. Surely, he pleads, society could have made better use of them?

His distinctive technical innovation was to use a new type of rhyme. In 1914 he wrote an experimental poem that begins:

Leaves
  Murmuring by myriads in the shimmering trees —
Lives
  Wakening with wonder in the Pyrenees.

He rhymes *leaves* with *lives*; instead of changing the last consonant of the rhyming syllable he changes the vowel. Though various Welsh, French and even English poets had used para-rhymes before, there is no evidence that Owen had ever read their poetry, and he probably invented the idea himself. These para-rhymes give many of his war poems — he does not, of course, use such rhymes always — a note of haunting melancholy that fits his tragic theme. In the solemn music of 'Strange Meeting' the incompleteness of the rhymes creates a sense of futility and emptiness as well as remoteness and darkness; they express the nightmare quality of the experience. However, the originality of his rhymes often conceals his other technical experiments; his poems use a wide variety of stanza forms and there is an increasing flexibility in his rhythms.

In insisting that Owen is a major poet one must stress

the range of his achievement. 'Miners' shows him feeling as strong a sympathy for coal-miners as for front-line troops; 'Exposure' stresses the nightmare cold and agony of trench warfare; 'Insensibility' and 'Greater Love' condemn the failures of the fortunate to sympathise with the unfortunate; 'Futility' and 'Strange Meeting' stress how much the world lost by letting its best young men be killed; 'Spring Offensive' and 'Dulce et Decorum Est' are vivid studies in realism, making clear that life and death in the front line were 'obscene as cancer' (to quote one of his letters) and not sweet and dignified as that safe civilian, Horace, had imagined them to be. These very different points are made in a language of sombre beauty, while the emotion that they communicate is intense, powerful and unselfish, for Owen's poetry expresses every soldier's indignation against modern war, and not the poet's private fear.

THE SEND-OFF

Down the close, darkening lanes they sang their way
To the siding-shed,
And lined the train with faces grimly gay.

Their breasts were stuck all white with wreath and spray
As men's are, dead.

Dull porters watched them, and a casual tramp
Stood staring hard,
Sorry to miss them from the upland camp.
Then, unmoved, signals nodded, and a lamp
Winked to the guard.   10

So secretly, like wrongs hushed-up, they went.
They were not ours:
We never heard to which front these were sent.

Nor there if they yet mock what women meant
Who gave them flowers.

Shall they return to beatings of great bells
In wild train-loads?
A few, a few, too few for drums and yells,
May creep back, silent, to still village wells
Up half-known roads.   20

SPRING OFFENSIVE

Halted against the shade of a last hill,
They fed, and lying easy, were at ease
And, finding comfortable chests and knees,
Carelessly slept. But many there stood still

To face the stark, blank sky beyond the ridge,
Knowing their feet had come to the end of the world.

Marvelling they stood, and watched the long grass swirled
By the May breeze, murmurous with wasp and midge,
For though the summer oozed into their veins
Like an injected drug for their bodies' pains,   10
Sharp on their souls hung the imminent line of grass,
Fearfully flashed the sky's mysterious glass.

Hour after hour they ponder the warm field —
And the far valley behind, where the buttercup
Had blessed with gold their slow boots coming up,
Where even the little brambles would not yield,
But clutched and clung to them like sorrowing hands;
They breathe like trees unstirred.

Till like a cold gust thrills the little word
At which each body and its soul begird   20
And tighten them for battle. No alarms
Of bugles, no high flags, no clamorous haste —
Only a lift and flare of eyes that faced
The sun, like a friend with whom their love is done.
O larger shone that smile against the sun, —
Mightier than His whose bounty these have spurned.

So, soon they topped the hill, and raced together
Over an open stretch of herb and heather
Exposed. And instantly the whole sky burned
With fury against them; earth set sudden cups   30
In thousands for their blood; and the green slope
Chasmed and steepened sheer to infinite space.

Of them who running on that last high place
Leapt to swift unseen bullets, or went up
On the hot blast and fury of hell's upsurge,
Or plunged and fell away past this world's verge,
Some say God caught them even before they fell.

But what say such as from existence' brink
Ventured but drove too swift to sink,
The few who rushed in the body to enter hell,   40
And there out-fiending all its fiends and flames
With superhuman inhumanities,
Long-famous glories, immemorial shames —
And crawling slowly back, have by degrees
Regained cool peaceful air in wonder —
Why speak not they of comrades that went under?

GREATER LOVE

RED lips are not so red
    As the stained stones kissed by the English dead.
Kindness of wooed and wooer
Seems shame to their love pure.
O Love, your eyes lose lure
    When I behold eyes blinded in my stead!

Your slender attitude
    Trembles not exquisite like limbs knife-skewed,
Rolling and rolling there
Where God seems not to care;   10
Till the fierce love they bear
    Cramps them in death's extreme decrepitude.

Your voice sings not so soft, —
    Though even as wind murmuring through raftered
        loft, —
Your dear voice is not dear,
Gentle, and evening clear,
As theirs whom none now hear,
    Now earth has stopped their piteous mouths that
        coughed.

Heart, you were never hot
    Nor large, not full like hearts made great with shot;   20

C

And though your hand be pale,
Paler are all which trail
Your cross through flame and hail:
Weep, you may weep, for you may touch them not.

ANTHEM FOR DOOMED YOUTH

WHAT passing-bells for these who die as cattle?
   Only the monstrous anger of the guns.
Only the stuttering rifles' rapid rattle
   Can patter out their hasty orisons.
No mockeries now for them; no prayers nor bells,
   Nor any voice of mourning save the choirs,—
The shrill, demented choirs of wailing shells;
   And bugles calling for them from sad shires.
What candles may be held to speed them all?
   Not in the hands of boys, but in their eyes   10
   Shall shine the holy glimmers of good-byes.
The pallor of girls' brows shall be their pall;
Their flowers the tenderness of patient minds,
And each slow dusk a drawing-down of blinds.

INSENSIBILITY

I

HAPPY are men who yet before they are killed
Can let their veins run cold.
Whom no compassion fleers
Or makes their feet
Sore on the alleys cobbled with their brothers.
The front line withers,
But they are troops who fade, not flowers
For poets' tearful fooling:
Men, gaps for filling:

Losses, who might have fought   10
Longer; but no one bothers.

II

And some cease feeling
Even themselves or for themselves.
Dullness best solves
The tease and doubt of shelling,
And Chance's strange arithmetic
Comes simpler than the reckoning of their shilling.
They keep no check on armies' decimation.

III

Happy are these who lose imagination:
They have enough to carry with ammunition.   20
Their spirit drags no pack,
Their old wounds, save with cold, can not more ache.
Having seen all things red,
Their eyes are rid
Of the hurt of the colour of blood for ever.
And terror's first constriction over,
Their hearts remain small-drawn.
Their senses in some scorching cautery of battle
Now long since ironed,
Can laugh among the dying, unconcerned.   30

IV

Happy the soldier home, with not a notion
How somewhere, every dawn, some men attack,
And many sighs are drained.
Happy the lad whose mind was never trained:
His days are worth forgetting more than not.
He sings along the march
Which we march taciturn, because of dusk,
The long, forlorn, relentless trend
From larger day to huger night.

V

We wise, who with a thought besmirch   40
Blood over all our soul,
How should we see our task
But through his blunt and lashless eyes?
Alive, he is not vital overmuch;
Dying, not mortal overmuch;
Nor sad, nor proud,
Nor curious at all.
He cannot tell
Old men's placidity from his.

VI

But cursed are dullards whom no cannon stuns,   50
That they should be as stones;
Wretched are they, and mean
With paucity that never was simplicity.
By choice they made themselves immune
To pity and whatever mourns in man
Before the last sea and the hapless stars;
Whatever mourns when many leave these shores;
Whatever shares
The eternal reciprocity of tears.

FUTILITY

Move him into the sun —
Gently its touch awoke him once,
At home, whispering of fields unsown.
Always it woke him, even in France,
Until this morning and this snow.
If anything might rouse him now
The kind old sun will know.

Think how it wakes the seeds,—
Woke, once, the clays of a cold star.
Are limbs, so dear-achieved, are sides,   10
Full-nerved — still warm — too hard to stir?
Was it for this the clay grew tall?
— O what made fatuous sunbeams toil
To break earth's sleep at all?

MINERS

THERE was a whispering in my hearth,
   A sigh of the coal,
Grown wistful of a former earth
   It might recall.

I listened for a tale of leaves
   And smothered ferns;
Frond-forests; and the low, sly lives
   Before the fawns.

My fire might show steam-phantoms simmer
   From Time's old cauldron,   10
Before the birds made nests in summer,
   Or men had children.

But the coals were murmuring of their mine,
   And moans down there
Of boys that slept wry sleep, and men
   Writhing for air.

And I saw white bones in the cinder-shard.
   Bones without number;
For many hearts with coal are charred
   And few remember.   20

I thought of some who worked dark pits
   Of war, and died

Digging the rock where Death reputes
   Peace lies indeed.

Comforted years will sit soft-chaired
   In rooms of amber;
The years will stretch their hands, well-cheered
   By our lives' ember.

The centuries will burn rich loads
   With which we groaned,   30
Whose warmth shall lull their dreaming lids
   While songs are crooned.
But they will not dream of us poor lads
   Lost in the ground.

AT A CALVARY NEAR THE ANCRE

ONE ever hangs where shelled roads part.
   In this war He too lost a limb,
But His disciples hide apart;
   And now the Soldiers bear with Him.

Near Golgotha strolls many a priest,
   And in their faces there is pride
That they were flesh-marked by the Beast
   By whom the gentle Christ's denied.

The scribes on all the people shove
   And bawl allegiance to the state,   10
But they who love the greater love
   Lay down their life; they do not hate.

INSPECTION

'You! What d'you mean by this?' I rapped.
'You dare come on parade like this?'
'Please, sir, it's —' ''Old yer mouth,' the sergeant snapped.
'I takes 'is name, sir?'—'Please, and then dismiss.'

Some days 'confined to camp' he got,
For being 'dirty on parade'.
He told me, afterwards, the damnèd spot
Was blood, his own. 'Well, blood is dirt,' I said.

'Blood's dirt,' he laughed, looking away
Far off to where his wound had bled   10
And almost merged for ever into clay.
'The world is washing out its stains,' he said.
'It doesn't like our cheeks so red:
Young blood's its great objection.
But when we're duly white-washed, being dead,
The race will bear Field-Marshal God's inspection.'

EXPOSURE

Our brains ache, in the merciless iced east winds that
        knive us. . . .
Wearied we keep awake because the night is silent. . . .
Low, drooping flares confuse our memory of the
        salient. . . .
Worried by silence, sentries whisper, curious, nervous,
    But nothing happens.

Watching, we hear the mad gusts tugging on the wire,
Like twitching agonies of men among its brambles.
Northward, incessantly, the flickering gunnery rumbles,

Far off, like a dull rumour of some other war.
   What are we doing here?   10

The poignant misery of dawn begins to grow. . . .
We only know war lasts, rain soaks, and clouds sag
      stormy.
Dawn massing in the east her melancholy army
Attacks once more in ranks on shivering ranks of gray,
   But nothing happens.

Sudden successive flights of bullets streak the silence.
Less deathly than the air that shudders black with snow,
With sidelong flowing flakes that flock, pause, and
      renew;
We watch them wandering up and down the wind's
      nonchalance,
   But nothing happens.   20

Pale flakes with fingering stealth come feeling for our
      faces —
We cringe in holes, back on forgotten dreams, and
      stare, snow-dazed,
Deep into grassier ditches. So we drowse, sun-dozed,
Littered with blossoms trickling where the blackbird
      fusses.
   Is it that we are dying?

Slowly our ghosts drag home: glimpsing the sunk fires,
      glozed
With crusted dark-red jewels: crickets jingle there;
For hours the innocent mice rejoice: the house is theirs;
Shutters and doors, all closed: on us the doors are
      closed,—
   We turn back to our dying.   30

Since we believe not otherwise can kind fires burn;
Nor ever suns smile true on child, or field, or fruit.
For God's invincible spring our love is made afraid;

Therefore, not loath, we lie out here; therefore were
    born,
  For love of God seems dying.

To-night, His frost will fasten on this mud and us,
Shrivelling many hands, puckering foreheads crisp.
The burying-party, picks and shovels in their shaking
    grasp,
Pause over half-known faces. All their eyes are ice,
  But nothing happens.   40

STRANGE MEETING

It seemed that out of battle I escaped
Down some profound dull tunnel, long since scooped
Through granites which titanic wars had groined.
Yet also there encumbered sleepers groaned,
Too fast in thought or death to be bestirred.
Then, as I probed them, one sprang up, and stared
With piteous recognition in fixed eyes,
Lifting distressful hands as if to bless.
And by his smile, I knew that sullen hall,
By his dead smile I knew we stood in Hell.   10
With a thousand pains that vision's face was grained;
Yet no blood reached there from the upper ground,
And no guns thumped, or down the flues made moan.
'Strange friend,' I said, 'here is no cause to mourn.'
'None,' said that other, 'save the undone years,
The hopelessness. Whatever hope is yours,
Was my life also; I went hunting wild
After the wildest beauty in the world,
Which lies not calm in eyes, or braided hair,
But mocks the steady running of the hour,   20
And if it grieves, grieves richlier than here.
For of my glee might many men have laughed,
And of my weeping something had been left,

Which must die now. I mean the truth untold,
The pity of war, the pity war distilled.
Now men will go content with what we spoiled,
Or, discontent, boil bloody, and be spilled.
They will be swift with swiftness of the tigress.
None will break ranks, though nations trek from progress.
Courage was mine, and I had mystery,   30
Wisdom was mine, and I had mastery:
To miss the march of this retreating world
Into vain citadels that are not walled.
Then, when much blood had clogged their chariot-
       wheels,
I would go up and wash them from sweet wells,
Even with truths that lie too deep for taint.
I would have poured my spirit without stint
But not through wounds; not on the cess of war.
Foreheads of men have bled where no wounds were.
I am the enemy you killed, my friend.   40
I knew you in this dark: for so you frowned
Yesterday through me as you jabbed and killed.
I parried; but my hands were loath and cold.
Let us sleep now. . . .'

T. S. ELIOT

ALTHOUGH Thomas Stearns Eliot (1888–1965) was born
in St. Louis, Missouri, and although he shows in *The Dry
Salvages* how powerfully he was affected by being brought
up beside the River Mississippi, his spiritual home was
New England. His family had lived there since the
seventeenth century when the god-fearing cordwainer,
Andrew Eliot, emigrated to Massachusetts from the
Somerset village of East Coker. The puritanism of New
England toughened his opinions on religion and literature
and reinforced his personal integrity and independence of
judgment. As a young man he studied philosophy and
Sanskrit at Harvard, and won scholarships to study in
Paris, Germany and Oxford. He found the cultural and
intellectual life of Europe so attractive that he settled in
England and eventually, in 1927, became a British citizen.
After teaching 'French, Latin, lower mathematics,
drawing, swimming, geography, history and baseball' in
the primary department of Highgate School in London,
and after holding various posts in banking and publishing,
he established himself as editor of a literary magazine,
The Criterion, and became a director of the publishing firm
of Faber and Faber. Meanwhile his reputation as a critic
and a poet was growing steadily on both sides of the
Atlantic, with the result that today no other modern poet
is so widely studied in universities, colleges and schools.

His early poems such as 'The Love Song of J. Alfred
Prufock' (1917), present fragmentary scenes from modern
urban life; their cumulative effect is to stress the in-
adequacy and purposelessness of many people's lives in this
century. Prufock's description of the dirty yellow fog,
rubbing its back along the window-panes as though it
were a lethargic cat, suggests that the speaker, and the
society he lives in, share the dreary, bored aimlessness of

the fog. The poem's central idea is that Prufock has lost faith in the real meaning of life; but instead of this being stated directly by the poet, it is suggested by Eliot's choice of metaphors and symbols.

The general idea has to be inferred from the parts: the words, or even sentences, that other writers would have used to link ideas, or to ease the transition from one idea to another, are omitted by Eliot, and the connections that he relies on are psychological rather than verbal or grammatical. In developing this technique he found that the only useful models were Ezra Pound, the Jacobean dramatists and — most of all — the French symbolist poets, especially Baudelaire and Laforgue; for he once said that: *The kind of poetry that I needed, to teach me the use of my own voice, did not exist in England at all; it was only found in the French.* He copied the symbolists' technique of using sceptical understatements to hint much more than they said outright, but he also found in the plays of Webster and Tourneur a useful model of how to devise a style that was both flexible and rhetorical.

There is an element of satire in 'The Love Song of J. Alfred Prufock' and in most of Eliot's early poems, and there are ironic undertones in the snatches of conversation by which the speakers in these poems give themselves away; but it would be wrong to place too much emphasis on the satire. Prufock is conscious of apocalyptic feelings and intuitions which it would be hopeless for him to try to express. He sees his predicament, though he fails to escape from it. Consequently we must see that Prufock appreciates the virtues that he cannot attain, and we must not regard him as merely grotesque or absurd.

'Whispers of Immortality' and 'Sweeney Among the Nightingales,' are interesting examples of the next period in Eliot's development. Like many of the other poems in his 1920 volume, they employ a terse, rather epigrammatic, quatrain, with the second and fourth lines rhyming. The rhythm has a strongly marked beat, and the emphatic rhymes give a finality to the stanza endings. Technically, these poems combine some of the qualities of the eight-

syllable lines written by Donne, and some of those of the
French nineteenth-century poet Gautier. Their technical
originality lies in the distinctive asperity that Eliot gives to
this traditional verse form. Eliot also takes other hints
from the methods of the French symbolist poets, such as
Verlaine, Laforgue and — especially — Corbière, whose
style has been described by a French encyclopaedia as
'clownesque', and whose tone has been summed up by an
American critic as 'scoffing realism'. The poems which
Eliot writes in this style tease or puzzle the reader, but
their symbols half-reveal a deep spiritual unhappiness
beneath the surface of Eliot's witty lines. He makes
important use of symmetrical contrasts, such as the
elaborate ones between Sweeney (an oafish, ape-like man
whom we meet in several of Eliot's poems) and
Agamemnon (the commander-in-chief of the Greek armies
attacking Troy), or between the attitudes to death of
Donne and those of the flippant Grishkin. But these
contrasts between the heroic or emotional past and the
unworthy or superficial present are not simple and clear-
cut, for, we are intended to have some human sympathy
for Sweeney and Grishkin, despite the dreariness of their
surroundings and the crudity of their feelings. Consequently, the attitudes which Eliot is seeking to evoke in his
reader are complex and ambivalent, for his subtle irony is
directed at very different targets simultaneously.

But having mastered these techniques, Eliot was not
content to go on using them, so in *The Waste Land* (1922) he
moved on to a different technique which was, in some
ways, a further development of that of 'The Love Song of
J. Alfred Prufock.' Apparently miscellaneous details are
accumulated so as to create a general impression of hopeless
fear and sterility; but the reader's erudition and instinctive,
emotional reactions have to supply links between the
seemingly separate images:

A rat crept softly through the vegetation
Dragging its slimy belly on the bank

While I was fishing in the dull canal
On a winter's evening round behind the gashouse
Musing upon the king my brother's wreck
And on the king my father's death before him.
White bodies naked on the low damp ground
And bones cast in a little low dry garret,
Rattled by the rat's foot only, year to year.
But at my back from time to time I hear
The sound of horns and motors, which shall bring
Sweeney to Mrs. Porter in the spring.

These lines rely on juxtaposition and contrast. They make us aware in turn of an ordinary rat by an ordinary canal, of Ferdinand in *The Tempest* thinking his father dead, of the Fisher King in a prehistoric fertility rite, of Actaeon surprising the naked Goddess of chastity, of Marvell's reminder to his Coy Mistress that life is short, and of Sweeney courting Mrs. Porter. Eliot is here collecting images that serve as examples to illustrate a general point that he never makes explicitly. He is content to let the psychological implications of his images suggest a unity: putting all his reliance on this process, he does not always use conventional logic to link his ideas, just as he does not always use conventional syntax to link his words. Consequently he demands a much greater intellectual effort from his readers than the Romantic poets had done. Although Eliot had learned much of this technique from his fellow American, Ezra Pound, and from the French symbolists whose poetry was colloquial and used contemporary images, nevertheless *The Waste Land* marked as decisive a turning-point in literary history as *Lyrical Ballads* had done in 1798. Eliot and Wordsworth criticised the respected poetry of the previous century; both began to write poetry near the time of a world war which intensified changes in literary and artistic taste.

One of Eliot's methods of exposing the sordidness of the present is to contrast a glimpse of it with a reminder of traditional culture. For instance, in order to show the

pettiness of the seduction of a typist by a house-agent's
clerk he introduces a parody of a sentimental little poem
by Goldsmith:

> *When lovely woman stoops to folly and*
> *Paces about her room again, alone,*
> *She smoothes her hair with automatic hand,*
> *And puts a record on the gramophone.*

Similarly, a fragment from Spenser — *Sweet Thames, run
softly till I end my song* — is followed by a picture of the
modern Thames with cigarette ends floating on it. To
react to such references the reader needs to have a very
wide background of knowledge — just as he does when
reading *Paradise Lost* — and Eliot is consciously writing for
a small, cultured minority prepared to make the effort of
discovering his meaning, since he believes that:

> Poets in our civilisation, as it exists at present, must be
> *difficult.* Our civilisation comprehends great variety and
> complexity, and this variety and complexity, playing
> upon a refined sensibility, must produce various and
> complex results. The poet must become more and more
> comprehensive, more allusive, more indirect.

It is easy to see why *The Waste Land* was at first in-
terpreted as an expression of post-war disillusion. Certainly
it reveals the lack of purpose and direction in the post-war
state of mind, and includes repulsive images of urban life,
which it juxtaposes with echoes of what is beautiful or
heroic. But *The Waste Land* is much more than a series of
variations on the theme of disillusion. It offers a whole-
range of themes and artistic innovations, and superimposes
upon its successive pictures of urban (usually London) life
a number of other 'actions'— for example, it refers
repeatedly to the tarot pack of cards and their symbolical
meanings, to the Gospels, to Hindu myths, and to
primitive fertility rites. The poem studies the growth and
decline of religious feeling in man, and his reactions to the

seasons. Eliot suggests similarities between primitive fertility myths, as investigated by anthropologists, and Christian teachings about the Resurrection. He also suggests similarities between the quest for salvation in London and the quest for the Grail in medieval legends. He attempts to create a technique that combines the *power of incantation in primitive poetry and music* with *the last subtle nuances of civilised feeling*. The resultant effect of the poem is well described by Northrop Frye: *Loveliness peeps fitfully through the squalor and an invisible divine presence haunts the misery of Europe.*

The impact of Eliot's startlingly new kind of poetry was re-inforced by the impact of his literary criticism which did much to create the taste by which his poetry came to be judged. This poetry was a reaction against the poetry of 'the last romantics', since it used a more flexible vocabulary and rhythm (that could be colloquial as well as rhetorical), and it also included a much wider range of topics (including apparently 'unpoetical' ones). Similarly his criticism exposed the weaknesses of romantic poetry. He contended that Romanticism overestimated the importance of the individual personality, believing that true religion and true culture both required the individual to adjust his personality to the claims of society and of tradition. He thought that the romantic spirit often made men selfish and anarchic. He wished to write poetry that carried on the tradition of poets such as Donne and Dryden who seemed important to him but who had been neglected by the Romantics.

We can summarise Eliot's critical beliefs by saying that he regarded an acute awareness of literary tradition as an essential part of one's reaction to contemporary literature. Feeling it his duty to defend the European cultural tradition, he summed up his opinions in 1928 with a touch of melodrama by announcing that he was *an Anglo-Catholic in religion, a classicist in literature, and a royalist in politics.* Even those who would disown Eliot's political and religious beliefs have come to pay great respect to his literary judgments, many of which (such as his admiration of Donne) have become widely accepted.

One of Eliot's main interests from 1930 onwards, and one of his most important achievements, was the writing of verse plays, on religious themes, that would nevertheless be contemporary in content and technique.

Meanwhile, he had also been devising new ways of writing religious poetry, just as his search for ways of writing plays in verse had also been a search for a new kind of religious drama. After *The Waste Land*, and then a few transitional poems such as *Ash Wednesday*, Eliot embarked on a constructive expression of his own faith in *Four Quartets* (1936-42), his last major work in the field of pure verse. In these four similar poems the transitions from idea to idea or from image to image are less violent than in the early poetry, and most of the difficulty of understanding them is due to the inherent difficulty of Eliot's subject-matter, and to the limitations of words as a medium of communication — a topic to which he keeps returning.

In turning to the writing of religious poetry, Eliot had to conquer a widespread prejudice against it. That he was so successful was a remarkable proof of his eminence in literature. But the writing of religious poetry raises the difficult question of whether a reader who is an atheist or an agnostic can appreciate it. I. A. Richards and T. S. Eliot believed that an atheist could appreciate religious poetry fully because poetry and religion were fundamentally different activities with different aims and functions. Accordingly the former asserted that *It is possible to have full literary or poetic appreciation without sharing the beliefs of the poet*, and Eliot asserted that *Poetry is no substitute for philosophy or theology or religion*. It seems probable, however, that they are overstating their case a little, and that one must have a degree of sympathy with the poet's ideas, or that at least Helen Gardner is right when she concludes: *It is not the poet's business to make us believe* what *he believes, but to make us believe* that *he believes*. If we are convinced of

Eliot's sincerity, we shall be impressed by the responsible, serious manner, and the courageously new technique, in which he discusses the major philosophical problems of this century.

WHISPERS OF IMMORTALITY

WEBSTER was much possessed by death
And saw the skull beneath the skin;
And breastless creatures under ground
Leaned backward with a lipless grin.

Daffodil bulbs instead of balls
Stared from the sockets of the eyes!
He knew that thought clings round dead limbs
Tightening its lusts and luxuries.

Donne, I suppose, was such another
Who found no substitute for sense,   10
To seize and clutch and penetrate;
Expert beyond experience,

He knew the anguish of the marrow
The ague of the skeleton;
No contact possible to flesh
Allayed the fever of the bone.

.   .   .   .

Grishkin is nice: her Russian eye
Is underlined for emphasis;
Uncorseted, her friendly bust
Gives promise of pneumatic bliss.   20

The couched Brazilian jaguar
Compels the scampering marmoset
With subtle effluence of cat;
Grishkin has a maisonette;

The sleek Brazilian Jaguar
Does not in its arboreal gloom
Distil so rank a feline smell
As Grishkin in a drawing-room.

> And even the Abstract Entities
> Circumambulate her charm;　　　　30
> But our lot crawls between dry ribs
> To keep our metaphysics warm.

SWEENEY AMONG THE NIGHTINGALES

ὤμοι, πέπληγμαι καιρίαν πληγὴν ἔσω.

APENECK Sweeney spreads his knees
Letting his arms hang down to laugh,
The zebra stripes along his jaw
Swelling to maculate giraffe.

The circles of the stormy moon
Slide westward toward the River Plate,
Death and the Raven drift above
And Sweeney guards the hornèd gate.

Gloomy Orion and the Dog
Are veiled; and hushed the shrunken seas;　　　10
The person in the Spanish cape
Tries to sit on Sweeney's knees

Slips and pulls the table cloth
Overturns a coffee-cup,
Reorganised upon the floor
She yawns and draws a stocking up;

The silent man in mocha brown
Sprawls at the window-sill and gapes;
The waiter brings in oranges
Bananas figs and hothouse grapes;　　　20

The silent vertebrate in brown
Contracts and concentrates, withdraws;
Rachel *née* Rabinovitch
Tears at the grapes with murderous paws;

She and the lady in the cape
Are suspect, thought to be in league;
Therefore the man with heavy eyes
Declines the gambit, shows fatigue,

Leaves the room and reappears
Outside the window, leaning in,   30
Branches of wistaria
Circumscribe a golden grin;

The host with someone indistinct
Converses at the door apart,
The nightingales are singing near
The Convent of the Sacred Heart,

And sang within the bloody wood
When Agamemnon cried aloud,
And let their liquid siftings fall
To stain the stiff dishonoured shroud.   40

THE DRY SALVAGES

I

I DO not know much about gods; but I think that the
    river
Is a strong brown god — sullen, untamed and
    intractable,
Patient to some degree, at first recognized as a frontier;
Useful, untrustworthy, as a conveyor of commerce;
Then only a problem confronting the builder of bridges.
The problem once solved, the brown god is almost
    forgotten
By dwellers in cities — ever, however, implacable,
Keeping his seasons and rages, destroyer, reminder
Of what men choose to forget. Unhonoured,
    unpropitiated

By worshippers of the machine, but waiting, watching
    and waiting.   10
His rhythm was present in the nursery bedroom.
In the rank ailanthus of the April dooryard,
In the smell of grapes on the autumn table,
And the evening circle in the winter gaslight.
The river is within us, the sea is all about us;
The sea is the land's edge also, the granite
Into which it reaches, the beaches where it tosses
Its hints of earlier and other creation:
The starfish, the hermit crab, the whale's backbone;
The pools where it offers to our curiosity   20
The more delicate algæ and the sea anemone.
It tosses up our losses, the torn seine,
The shattered lobsterpot, the broken oar
And the gear of foreign dead men. The sea has many
    voices,
Many gods and many voices.

                    The salt is on the briar rose,
The fog is in the fir trees.
             The sea howl
And the sea yelp, are different voices
Often together heard: the whine in the rigging,
The menace and caress of wave that breaks on water,
The distant rota in the granite teeth,   30
And the wailing warning from the approaching
    headland
Are all sea voices, and the heaving groaner
Rounded homewards, and the seagull:
And under the oppression of the silent fog
The tolling bell
Measures time not our time, rung by the unhurried
Ground swell, a time
Older than the time of chronometers, older
Than time counted by anxious worried mothers
Lying awake, calculating the future,   40
Trying to unweave, unwind, unravel
And piece together the past and the future

Between midnight and dawn, when the past is all
    deception,
The future futureless, before the morning watch
When time stops and time is never ending;
And the ground swell, that is and was from the
    beginning,
Clangs
The bell.

II

Where is there an end of it, the soundless wailing,
The silent withering of autumn flowers   50
Dropping their petals and remaining motionless;
Where is there an end to the drifting wreckage,
The prayer of the bone on the beach, the unprayable
Prayer at the calamitous annunciation?

There is no end, but addition: the trailing
Consequence of further days and hours,
While emotion takes to itself the emotionless
Years of living among the breakage
Of what was believed in as the most reliable —
And therefore the fittest for renunciation.   60

There is the final addition, the failing
Pride or resentment at failing powers,
The unattached devotion which might pass for
    devotionless,
In a drifting boat with a slow leakage,
The silent listening to the undeniable
Clamour of the bell of the last annunciation.

Where is the end of them, the fishermen sailing
Into the wind's tail, where the fog cowers?
We cannot think of a time that is oceanless
Or of an ocean not littered with wastage   70
Or of a future that is not liable
Like the past, to have no destination.

We have to think of them as forever bailing,
Setting and hauling, while the North East lowers
Over shallow banks unchanging and erosionless
Or drawing their money, drying sails at dockage;
Not as making a trip that will be unpayable
For a haul that will not bear examination.

There is no end of it, the voiceless wailing,
No end to the withering of withered flowers,   80
To the movement of pain that is painless and
        motionless,
To the drift of the sea and the drifting wreckage,
The bone's prayer to Death its God. Only the hardly,
        barely prayable
Prayer of the one Annunciation.

It seems, as one becomes older,
That the past has another pattern, and ceases to be a
        mere sequence —
Or even development: the latter a partial fallacy
Encouraged by superficial notions of evolution,
Which becomes, in the popular mind, a means of
        disowning the past.
The moments of happiness — not the sense of well-being, 90
Fruition, fulfilment, security or affection,
Or even a very good dinner, but the sudden
        illumination —
We had the experience, but missed the meaning,
And approach to the meaning restores the experience
In a different form, beyond any meaning
We can assign to happiness. I have said before
That the past experience revived in the meaning
Is not the experience of one life only
But of many generations — not forgetting
Something that is probably quite ineffable: 100
The backward look behind the assurance
Of recorded history, the backward half-look
Over the shoulder, towards the primitive terror.

Now, we come to discover that the moments of agony
(Whether, or not, due to misunderstanding,
Having hoped for the wrong things or dreaded the
          wrong things,
Is not in question) are likewise permanent
With such permanence as time has. We appreciate
          this better
In the agony of others, nearly experienced,
Involving ourselves, than in our own.   110
For our own past is covered by the currents of action,
But the torment of others remains an experience
Unqualified, unworn by subsequent attrition.
People change, and smile: but the agony abides.
Time the destroyer is time the preserver,
Like the river with its cargo of dead negroes, cows and
          chicken coops,
The bitter apple and bite in the apple.
And the ragged rock in the restless waters,
Waves wash over it, fogs conceal it;
On a halcyon day it is merely a monument,   120
In navigable weather it is always a seamark
To lay a course by: but in the sombre season
Or the sudden fury, is what it always was.

III

I sometimes wonder if that is what Krishna meant —
Among other things — or one way of putting the same
          thing:
That the future is a faded song, a Royal Rose or a
          lavender spray
Of wistful regret for those who are not yet here to regret,
Pressed between yellow leaves of a book that has never
          been opened.
And the way up is the way down, the way forward is the
          way back.
You cannot face it steadily, but this thing is sure,   130
That time is no healer: the patient is no longer here.
When the train starts, and the passengers are settled

To fruit, periodicals and business letters
(And those who saw them off have left the platform)
Their faces relax from grief into relief,
To the sleepy rhythm of a hundred hours.
Fare forward, travellers! not escaping from the past
Into different lives, or into any future;
You are not the same people who left the station
Or who will arrive at any terminus,   140
While the narrowing rails slide together behind you;
And on the deck of the drumming liner
Watching the furrow that widens behind you,
You shall not think 'the past is finished'
Or 'the future is before us'.
At nightfall, in the rigging and the aerial,
Is a voice descanting (though not to the ear,
The murmuring shell of time, and not in any language)
'Fare forward, you who think that you are voyaging;
You are not those who saw the harbour   150
Receding, or those who will disembark,
Here between the hither and the farther shore
While time is withdrawn, consider the future
And the past with an equal mind.
At the moment which is not of action or inaction
You can receive this: "on whatever sphere of being
The mind of men may be intent
At the time of death"— that is the one action
(And the time of death is every moment)
Which shall fructify in the lives of others: 160
And do not think of the fruit of action.
Fare forward.

           O voyagers, O seamen,
You who come to port, and you whose bodies
Will suffer the trial and judgment of the sea,
Or whatever event, this is your real destination.'
So Krishna, as when he admonished Arjuna
On the field of battle.
               Not fare well,
But fare forward, voyagers.

IV

Lady, whose shrine stands on the promontory,
Pray for all those who are in ships, those   170
Whose business has to do with fish, and
Those concerned with every lawful traffic
And those who conduct them.
Repeat a prayer also on behalf of
Women who have seen their sons or husbands
Setting forth and not returning:
Figlia del tuo figlio,
Queen of Heaven.
Also pray for those who were in ships, and
Ended their voyage on the sand, in the sea's lips   180
Or in the dark throat which will not reject them
Or wherever cannot reach them the sound of the sea
        bell's
Perpetual angelus.

V

To communicate with Mars, converse with spirits,
To report the behaviour of the sea monster,
Describe the horoscope, haruspicate or scry,
Observe disease in signatures, evoke
Biography from the wrinkles of the palm
And tragedy from fingers; release omens
By sortilege, or tea leaves, riddle the inevitable   190
With playing cards, fiddle with pentagrams
Or barbituric acids, or dissect
The recurrent image into pre-conscious terrors —
To explore the womb, or tomb, or dreams; all these are
        usual
Pastimes and drugs, and features of the press:
And always will be, some of them especially
When there is distress of nations and perplexity
Whether on the shores of Asia, or in the Edgeware Road.
Men's curiosity searches past and future

And clings to that dimension. But to apprehend   200
The point of intersection of the timeless
With time, is an occupation for the saint —
No occupation either, but something given
And taken, in a lifetime's death in love,
Ardour and selflessness and self-surrender.
For most of us, there is only the unattended
Moment, the moment in and out of time,
The distraction fit, lost in a shaft of sunlight,
The wild thyme unseen, or the winter lightning
Or the waterfall, or music heard so deeply   210
That it is not heard at all, but you are the music
While the music lasts. These are only hints and guesses,
Hints followed by guesses; and the rest
Is prayer, observance, discipline, thought and action.
The hint half-guessed, the gift half-understood, is
          Incarnation.
Here the impossible union
Of spheres of existence is actual,
Here the past and future
Are conquered, and reconciled,
Where action were otherwise movement   220
Of that which is only moved
And has in it no source of movement —
Driven by daemonic, chthonic
Powers. And right action is freedom
From past and future also.
For most of us, this is the aim
Never here to be realised;
Who are only undefeated
Because we have gone on trying;
We, content at the last   230
If our temporal reversion nourish
(Not too far from the yew-tree)
The life of significant soil.

SIR JOHN BETJEMAN

Sir John, who became Poet Laureate in 1972, begins his
'Distant View of a Provincial Town' with these lines:

> *Beside those spires so spick and span*
> *Against an unencumbered sky*
> *The old Great Western Railway ran*
> *When someone different was I.*

> *St. Aidan's with the prickly knobs*
> *And iron spikes and coloured tiles —*
> *Where Auntie Maud devoutly bobs*
> *In those enriched vermilion aisles.*

There are some reasons for doubting whether this is
poetry at all. The thumping rhythm is obvious, the metre
is one we associate with hymns or comic verse, the rhymes
(such as *knobs* and *bobs*) are a little comic, and the use of
colloquialisms such as 'prickly knobs' is obviously chatty.
In such verse Betjeman is resolved to describe this
provincial town as it was in the past, and to recall the
emotions he felt as a boy; unlike Auden or Eliot, he is not
describing the present.

But perhaps this is not the whole truth and there are
genuine qualities in this verse after all. It expresses
accurately an attitude to the recent past that is at once
individual to Betjeman and typical of a class. Many
middle-aged members of the middle-class look back with
nostalgia to an age when taxes were low and servants
plentiful, when churches were full and the un-nationalised
railways were fascinating, when the countryside was
unspoilt and when the sun never set on the British Empire.
Many young people who never remember such an age
believe that it existed and that they have missed something
by not having lived in it. Betjeman's verse expresses this
attitude for them neatly and memorably.

John Betjeman's birth, upbringing and education fitted
him admirably to be the spokesman of nostalgic middle-
class attitudes. His prosperous father, whose family had
come from Holland in the eighteenth century, owned a
factory in Islington. John was born in 1906 in the borough
of St. Pancras, on the edge of Parliament Hill Fields, when
it was still fashionable to have a town house near to the
centre of London. His father also owned land in Cornwall,
near the beach which he describes in 'Greenaway', and his
childhood was spent either there or in Highgate. As a pupil
at Highgate Junior School he solemnly made a selection
of 'The Best Poems of Betjeman' and presented them to
'The American master', a Mr. T. S. Eliot. He then went to
Marlborough, where he was terrified by bullies and
taunted with being a German spy, and on to Oxford, where
he enjoyed the champagne breakfasts and parties. He
developed very different friendships and enthusiasms from
those that W. H. Auden was developing in the same
university at the same time. But he did not get on with his
tutor, the distinguished scholar, C. S. Lewis, and he left
after failing his examination in 'Holy Scripture'.

Gradually he achieved fame as a writer, and then as a
television personality. His *Collected Poems*, published in
1958, and his autobiographical poem, *Summoned by
Bells*, sold so many copies and made so much money that
most critics have doubted whether he is a genuine poet,
and have labelled his admirers as gullible. John Wain
has insisted that his popularity is *one more sign that the
middle-brow public distrusts and fears poetry*. On the
other hand his confessed admirers include Philip Larkin
and W. H. Auden, who has edited an American edition
of his poems under the title of *Slick but not Streamlined*.
When he was made Poet Laureate, his appointment was
welcomed by both scholars and the general public; and
when Betjeman died in May 1984, Philip Larkin
summed up the view of many other people when he said
that 'He was not only the best-loved poet, but one of the
best-loved men of our time.'

As a poet, and as a television lecturer, Betjeman was a persuasive interpreter of the past that is still with us or has only just disappeared. He writes lovingly about towns where *the old Great Western Railway ran* before it was nationalised and renamed — perhaps even closed. His topics include many things that most people consider prosaic or even ugly, because they have not been out of fashion for very long, and he once said: *I love suburbs and gas-lights and Gothic-revival churches and mineral railways, provincial towns and garden cities.* He is very interested in the best examples of Victorian architecture, which were formerly thought pretentious but are now beginning to seem quaint — or even beautiful.

He condemns the new ugliness and vandalism of the twentieth century, but forgives the ugliness of the nineteenth century, such as that of *Chapels of ease by railway lines.* This affectionate knowledge of architecture makes him a connoisseur of the buildings and architectural trivia that the past (especially the recent past) has contributed to the present, or which the present is quickly making out of date. As new television masts or skyscraper blocks of flats rise higher and higher, the sky beside St. Aidan's spires is no longer 'unencumbered', but the spires become dearer and dearer to Betjeman. When he writes or talks of such buildings, he combines his knowledge of their architectural history with sympathetic insight into the people such as Auntie Maud who are associated with them.

His interest in the Church of England was detailed and profound. He was an expert on its ritual; and if he laughed at its futilities or failures, it is with sincere affection. Most of all he was an authority on architecture. He partly wrote, partly edited, Collins's *Guide to English Parish Churches*, and he gave gripping talks on television about the beauties of English churches.

As a poet one of his best qualities is a sense of place. The places he writes about appeal to him chiefly because of their associations, because they take him back to the happier moments of his boyhood. The landmarks that seem most beautiful to him in the present are those that commemorate the disappearing past; he knows them so well that in writing about them he is indirectly writing his autobiography. He paints the particular details of recognisable landscapes, whether his subjects are the rocky cliffs of Cornwall or the declining inner suburbs of some Victorian town; consequently his poems portray a wide variety of landscapes, especially of landscapes utterly neglected by other poets.

However, his poetry has things to say on other topics besides the past, architecture, and the Church of England. He is especially successful in achieving a simultaneous expression of nostalgia and terror, for like Dr. Johnson he has a savage terror of death which sometimes overwhelms him with melancholy and is only partly alleviated by his religious convictions. In 'Greenaway' he gives us the vivid sensation of a nightmare in which he cannot swim back to shore; 'Before the Anaesthetic' is a serious poem in which he lies in bed before an operation and is filled with so acute a fear of death that he temporarily loses faith in God; 'N.W.5 and N.6' gives us a convincing account of how as a young boy he caught from a sadistic nurse an urgent fear of going to hell; and 'Death in Leamington', which describes the unnoticed death of an old woman in a house where the stucco has begun to peel off, unites technical skill and lightness of touch with serious comments on the self-centred nature of modern living.

An emotion which he does not always express success-fully is anger. His poem 'In Westminster Abbey' exposes the unimaginative selfishness of an upper-class woman in war-time:

> *Gracious Lord, oh bomb the Germans.*
> *Spare their women for Thy Sake. . . .*

He is too amused to be bitterly angry, and so is successful — in a deliberately limited way. 'Come, friendly bombs, and fall on Slough' is a short, effective outburst against the treeless ugliness of new factory-towns such as Slough. But longer poems that attempt indignation such as 'The Town

Clerk's Views' and 'The Dear Old Village' are less convincing essays in sarcasm. The latter poem is almost saved by its wit, but it resists too many changes to be intelligent. It makes its points cleverly, ridiculing the urban nature of the education that some country children receive when they leave their village school at eleven-plus:

> *The children have a motor-bus instead,*
> *And in a town eleven miles away*
> *We train them to be 'Citizens of Today'.*
> *And many a cultivated hour they pass*
> *In a fine school with walls of vita-glass.*
> *Civics, eurhythmics, economics, Marx,*
> *How – to – respect – wild – life – in – National – Parks;*
> *Plastics, gymnastics — thus they learn to scorn*
> *The old thatch'd cottages where they were born.*

In these lines Betjeman ridicules the jargon of modern education and its tendency to train pupils for town life instead of country life, but the effect of his telling arguments is muffled by his feudal assumption that these children ought still to be trained to touch their forelock to the squire; Betjeman forgets how poor and underprivileged were those who lived in 'the old thatch'd cottages' that he idealises. He is more successful as a satirist in poems such as 'The Village Inn' where he attacks fewer targets at one time, and where the virtues whose disappearance he mourns are genuine.

The reader's main problem is how seriously to take Betjeman. His poetry is a strange mixture of humour and lyricism. Usually he does not mean it to be as funny as it could be made to seem. His apparent flippancy is often the mock-modesty of a shy man who hides his deepest feelings behind a shallow joke. If he often makes fun of upper-middle-class attitudes, he does it from inside; he gives the impression that he is keeping the joke well inside the family. To return to the example with which we began — he is too fond of Auntie Maud to press the joke against her religious enthusiasms very far.

UPPER LAMBOURNE

Up the ash-tree climbs the ivy,
    Up the ivy climbs the sun,
With a twenty-thousand pattering
    Has a valley breeze begun,
Feathery ash, neglected elder,
    Shift the shade and make it run —

Shift the shade towards the nettles,
    And the nettles set it free
To streak the stained Carrara headstone
    Where, in nineteen-twenty-three,   10
He who trained a hundred winners
    Paid the Final Entrance Fee.

Leathery limbs of Upper Lambourne,
    Leathery skin from sun and wind,
Leathery breeches, spreading stables,
    Shining saddles left behind —
To the down the string of horses
    Moving out of sight and mind.

Feathery ash in leathery Lambourne
    Waves above the sarsen stone,   20
And Edwardian plantations
    So coniferously moan
As to make the swelling downland,
    Far-surrounding, seem their own.

YOUTH AND AGE ON BEAULIEU RIVER, HANTS

EARLY sun on Beaulieu water
   Lights the undersides of oaks,
Clumps of leaves it floods and blanches,
All transparent glow the branches
   Which the double sunlight soaks;
To her craft on Beaulieu water
Clemency the General's daughter
   Pulls across with even strokes.

Schoolboy-sure she is this morning;
   Soon her sharpie's rigg'd and free.   10
Cool beneath a garden awning
   Mrs. Fairclough, sipping tea
And raising large long-distance glasses
As the little sharpie passes,
   Sighs our sailor girl to see:

Tulip figure, so appealing,
   Oval face, so serious-eyed,
Tree-roots passed and muddy beaches.
On to huge and lake-like reaches,
   Soft and sun-warm, see her glide —   20
Slacks the slim young limbs revealing,
Sun-brown arm the tiller feeling —
   With the wind and with the tide.

Evening light will bring the water,
   Day-long sun will burst the bud,
Clemency, the General's daughter,
   Will return upon the flood.
But the older woman only
Knows the ebb-tide leaves her lonely,
   With the shining fields of mud.   30

VERSES TURNED IN AID OF A
PUBLIC SUBSCRIPTION (1952)
TOWARDS THE RESTORATION OF THE CHURCH OF
ST. KATHERINE CHISELHAMPTON, OXON

ACROSS the wet November night
The church is bright with candlelight
    And waiting Evensong.
A single bell with plaintive strokes
Pleads louder than the stirring oaks
    The leafless lanes along.

It calls the choirboys from their tea
And villagers, the two or three,
    Damp down the kitchen fire,
Let out the cat, and up the lane   10
Go paddling through the gentle rain
    Of misty Oxfordshire.

How warm the many candles shine
On Samuel Dowbiggin's design
    For this interior neat,
These high box pews of Georgian days
Which screen us from the public gaze
    When we make answer meet;

How gracefully their shadow falls
On bold pilasters down the walls   20
    And on the pulpit high.
The chandeliers would twinkle gold
As pre-Tractarian sermons roll'd
    Doctrinal, sound and dry.

From that west gallery no doubt
The viol and serpent tooted out

The Tallis tune to Ken,
And firmly at the end of prayers
The clerk below the pulpit stairs
   Would thunder out 'Amen'.   30

But every wand'ring thought will cease
Before the noble altarpiece,
   With carven swags array'd,
For there in letters all may read
The Lord's Commandments, Prayer and Creed,
   And decently display'd.

On country mornings sharp and clear
The penitent in faith draw near
   And kneeling here below
Partake the Heavenly Banquet spread   40
Of Sacramental Wine and Bread
   And Jesus' presence know.

And must that plaintive bell in vain
Plead loud along the dripping lane?
   And must the building fall?
Not while we love the Church and live
And of our charity will give
   Our much, our more, our all.

CHURCH OF ENGLAND THOUGHTS

OCCASIONED BY HEARING THE BELLS OF MAGDALEN
TOWER FROM THE BOTANIC GARDEN, OXFORD,
ON ST. MARY MAGDALEN'S DAY

I SEE the urn against the yew,
   The sunlit urn of sculptured stone,
I see its shapely shadow fall
On this enormous garden wall
   Which makes a kingdom of its own

A grassy kingdom sweet to view
  With tiger lilies still in flower
And beds of umbelliferae
Ranged in Linnaean symmetry,
  All in the sound of Magdalen tower.   10

A multiplicity of bells,
  A changing cadence, rich and deep
Swung from those pinnacles on high
To fill the trees and flood the sky
  And rock the sailing clouds to sleep.

A Church of England sound, it tells
  Of 'moderate worship, God and State,'
Where matins congregations go
Conservative and good and slow
  To elevations of the plate.   20

And loud through resin-scented chines
  And purple rhododendrons roll'd,
I hear the bells for Eucharist
From churches blue with incense mist
  Where reredoses twinkle gold.

Chapels-of-ease by railway lines
  And humble streets and smells of gas
I hear your plaintive ting-tangs call
From many a gabled western wall
  To Morning Prayer or Holy Mass.   30

In country churches old and pale
  I hear the changes smoothly rung
And watch the coloured sallies fly
From rugged hands to rafters high
  As round and back the bells are swung.

Before the spell begin to fail,
  Before the bells have lost their power,

Before the grassy kingdom fade
And Oxford traffic roar invade,
   I thank the bells of Magdalen Tower.   40

CHRISTMAS

THE bells of waiting Advent ring,
   The Tortoise stove is lit again
And lamp-oil light across the night
   Has caught the streaks of winter rain
In many a stained-glass window sheen
From Crimson Lake to Hooker's Green.

The holly in the windy hedge
   And round the Manor House the yew
Will soon be stripped to deck the ledge,
   The altar, font and arch and pew,   10
So that the villagers can say
'The church looks nice' on Christmas Day.

Provincial public houses blaze
   And Corporation tramcars clang,
On lighted tenements I gaze
   Where paper decorations hang,
And bunting in the red Town Hall
Says 'Merry Christmas to you all.'

And London shops on Christmas Eve
   Are strung with silver bells and flowers   20
As hurrying clerks the City leave
   To pigeon-haunted classic towers,
And marbled clouds go scudding by
The many-steepled London sky.

And girls in slacks remember Dad,
   And oafish louts remember Mum,

And sleepless children's hearts are glad,
　And Christmas-morning bells say 'Come!'
Even to shining ones who dwell
Safe in the Dorchester Hotel.　　　　　　30

And is it true? And is it true,
　This most tremendous tale of all,
Seen in a stained-glass window's hue,
　A Baby in an ox's stall?
The Maker of the stars and sea
Become a Child on earth for me?

And is it true? For if it is,
　No loving fingers tying strings
Around those tissued fripperies,
　The sweet and silly Christmas things,　　40
Bath salts and inexpensive scent
And hideous tie so kindly meant,

No love that in a family dwells,
　No carolling in frosty air,
Nor all the steeple-shaking bells
　Can with this single Truth compare —
That God was Man in Palestine
And lives today in Bread and Wine.

THE VILLAGE INN

'THE village inn, the dear old inn,
So ancient, clean and free from sin,
True centre of our rural life
Where Hodge sits down beside his wife
And talks of Marx and nuclear fission
With all a rustic's intuition.
Ah, more than church or school or hall,
The village inn's the heart of all.'

So spake the brewer's P.R.O.,
A man who really ought to know,   10
For he is paid for saying so.
And then he kindly gave to me
A lovely coloured booklet free.
'Twas full of prose that sang the praise
Of coaching inns in Georgian days,
Showing how public-houses are
More modern than the motor-car,
More English than the weald or wold
And almost equally as old,
And run for love and not for gold   20
Until I felt a filthy swine
For loathing beer and liking wine,
And rotten to the very core
For thinking village inns a bore,
And village bores more sure to roam
To village inns than stay at home.
And then I thought I *must* be wrong,
So up I rose and went along
To that old village alehouse where
In neon lights is written 'Bear'.   30

Ah, where's the inn that once I knew
    With brick and chalky wall
Up which the knobbly pear-tree grew
    For fear the place would fall?

Oh, that old pot-house isn't there,
    It wasn't worth our while;
You'll find we have rebuilt 'The Bear'
    In Early Georgian style.

But winter jasmine used to cling
    With golden stars a-shine   40
Where rain and wind would wash and swing
    The crudely painted sign.

And where's the roof of golden thatch?
  The chimney-stack of stone?
The crown-glass panes that used to match
  Each sunset with their own?

Oh now the walls are red and smart,
  The roof has emerald tiles.
The neon sign's a work of art
  And visible for miles.   50

The bar inside was papered green,
  The settles grained like oak,
The only light was paraffin,
  The woodfire used to smoke.

And photographs from far and wide
  Were hung around the room:
The hunt, the church, the football side,
  And Kitchener of Khartoum.

Our air-conditioned bars are lined
  With washable material,   60
The stools are steel, the taste refined,
  Hygienic and ethereal.

Hurrah, hurrah, for hearts of oak!
  Away with inhibitions!
For here's a place to sit and soak
  In sanit'ry conditions.

GREENAWAY

I KNOW so well this turfy mile,
  These clumps of sea-pink withered brown,
The breezy cliff, the awkward stile,
  The sandy path that takes me down

To crackling layers of broken slate
    Where black and flat sea-woodlice crawl
And isolated rock pools wait
    Wash from the highest tides of all.

I know the roughly blasted track
    That skirts a small and smelly bay   10
And over squelching bladder-wrack
    Leads to the beach at Greenaway.

Down on the shingle safe at last
    I hear the slowly dragging roar
As mighty rollers mount to cast
    Small coal and seaweed on the shore.

And spurting far as it can reach
    The shooting surf comes hissing round
To leave a line along the beach
    Of cowries waiting to be found.   20

Tide after tide by night and day
    The breakers battle with the land
And rounded smooth along the bay
    The faithful rocks protecting stand.

But in a dream the other night,
    I saw this coastline from the sea
And felt the breakers plunging white
    Their weight of waters over me.

There were the stile, the turf, the shore,
    The safety line of shingle beach;   30
With every stroke I struck the more
    The backwash sucked me out of reach.

Back into what a water-world
    Of waving weed and waiting claws?
Of writhing tentacles uncurled
    To drag me to what dreadful jaws?

HERTFORDSHIRE

I HAD forgotten Hertfordshire,
　　The large unwelcome fields of roots
Where with my knickerbockered sire
　　I trudged in syndicated shoots;

And that unlucky day when I
　　Fired by mistake into the ground
Under a Lionel Edwards sky
　　And felt disapprobation round.

The slow drive home by motor-car,
　　A heavy Rover Landaulette,　　　　　　　　10
Through Welwyn, Hatfield, Potters Bar,
　　Tweed and cigar smoke, gloom and wet:

'How many times must I explain
　　The way a boy should hold a gun?'
I recollect my father's pain
　　At such a milksop for a son.

And now I see these fields once more
　　Clothed, thank the Lord, in summer green,
Pale corn waves rippling to a shore
　　The shadowy cliffs of elm between,　　　　　　20

Colour-washed cottages reed-thatched
　　And weather-boarded water mills,
Flint churches, brick and plaster patched,
　　On mildly undistinguished hills —

They still are there. But now the shire
　　Suffers a devastating change,
Its gentle landscape strung with wire,
　　Old places looking ill and strange.

One can't be sure where London ends,
   New towns have filled the fields of root   30
Where father and his business friends
   Drove in the Landaulette to shoot;

Tall concrete standards line the lane,
   Brick boxes glitter in the sun:
Far more would these have caused him pain
   Than my mishandling of a gun.

DEATH IN LEAMINGTON

SHE died in the upstairs bedroom
   By the light of the ev'ning star
That shone through the plate glass window
   From over Leamington Spa.

Beside her the lonely crochet
   Lay patiently and unstirred,
But the fingers that would have work'd it
   Were dead as the spoken word.

And Nurse came in with the tea-things
   Breast high 'mid the stands and chairs —   10
But Nurse was alone with her own little soul,
   And the things were alone with theirs.

She bolted the big round window,
   She let the blinds unroll,
She set a match to the mantle,
   She covered the fire with coal.

And 'Tea!' she said in a tiny voice,
   'Wake up! It's nearly *five*.'
Oh! Chintzy, chintzy cheeriness,
   Half dead and half alive!   20

Do you know that the stucco is peeling?
  Do you know that the heart will stop?
From those yellow Italianate arches
  Do you hear the plaster drop?

Nurse looked at the silent bedstead,
  At the gray decaying face,
As the calm of a Leamington ev'ning
  Drifted into the place.

She moved the table of bottles
  Away from the bed to the wall;   30
And tiptoeing gently over the stairs
  Turned down the gas in the hall.

W. H. AUDEN

W.H. Auden (1907-1973) once seemed a Marxist poet. He was sympathetic to the idealist aims of the Communist party, though he never joined it. He wanted the liberals and Socialists in each country to form a Popular Front with the Communists to resist the Fascists at home and abroad. In domestic politics, he condemned the British government for doing so little to help the two or three millions who were unemployed. In international affairs, the crisis of his generation came when Franco, helped by Hitler and Mussolini, began a civil war against the Popular Front government in Spain, which had been elected democratically. Auden thought that Britain and France ought to have intervened to save the Spanish government, although he saw clearly that the Communists took an increasingly selfish part in running the war as it dragged on. He believed that if western man was to save himself from a global disaster by political methods, then the Spanish war was the last chance to do so:

> *We are left alone with our day and the time is short and*
> > *History to the defeated*
> *May say Alas but cannot help or pardon.*

To win support for such important causes he felt it his duty to disturb the complacency of the upper middle class from which he sprang, and to try to bridge the gulf between it and the workers.

Consequently, he felt slightly ashamed of his privileged upbringing. He had been born at York in 1907. Soon afterwards his father became Professor of Public Health at Birmingham University. From 1915 to 1920 Auden went to St. Edmund's preparatory school, where he met Christopher Isherwood — who later collaborated with him in writing verse plays and emigrated to America with him. From 1920 to 1925 he was a pupil at a public school, Gresham's School, Holt; from 1925 to 1928 he was an undergraduate at Christ Church, Oxford. Here he became the leader of a group of writers — Isherwood, Spender, MacNeice, Cecil Day Lewis and Rex Warner. Rarely has a poet been so widely imitated by his contemporaries; rarely has a poet written so easily and so fast; rarely has one been so absorbed in social and political problems.

After graduating and leaving Oxford, Auden went for a year (1928–9) to Berlin, just before Hitler seized power. He was thrilled by German culture, especially the plays of Bertolt Brecht, some of whose techniques he later copied in his verse plays. He was attracted by the psychology of Freud's German disciples, and became convinced that illness was caused by a sense of guilt. Ever since those days he has continued to think of the poet's function as that of psycho-analysing society, and his poetry is full of psychiatric terminology. At the time when he went to Germany his fundamentally religious mind was attracted by those parts of the teaching of Marx and Freud in which their genius had isolated — and then over-emphasised — ideas that are fundamentally Christian. Not understanding the real reason why these ideas attracted him, he announced his conversion to atheism, but he continued to probe the nature of man's evil, using the techniques of Freudian and Marxist analysis for a fundamentally Christian purpose.

In 1930 Auden returned to Britain, and published his first volume of poems, which at once attracted notice. For the next five years he taught as a schoolmaster at Larchfield Academy, Helensburgh (Scotland) and the Downs School, Colwall (near Malvern). He then worked for six months with the G.P.O. film unit, writing his poem *Night Mail* as a commentary for a film. He and Louis MacNeice visited Iceland in 1936; on returning they published *Letters from Iceland*, which includes his entertaining *Letter to Lord Byron*. In 1937 he went to Spain during the Civil War. In 1938 he and Isherwood decided to journey to another war, and went to China (then invaded by the Japanese).

On both the outward and return journeys, they crossed the United States, which attracted them so strongly that in 1939 they emigrated to the States. In explanation of this decision Auden said: *The attractiveness of America to a writer is its openness and lack of tradition. You are forced to live. There is no past.* In European politics his great hope had been that the liberal-minded people in all countries would unite to stop the march of Fascism before Hitler became so powerful that this could not be done without precipitating a second world war. Since by the time of Munich this opportunity had been missed, Auden became less absorbed in politics: the void in his intellectual life was filled by two new interests — theology and opera.

The poetry that Auden wrote up to this point in his life gave remarkable evidence of his versatility and fluency. Some of it expressed Marxist criticisms of society, but his best poetry stopped short of propaganda and remained true to the principle that he proclaimed in his introduction to his anthology, *The Poet's Tongue*:

> Poetry is not concerned with telling people what to do, but with extending our knowledge of good and evil, perhaps making the necessity for action more urgent and its nature more clear, but only leading us to the point where it is possible for us to make a rational and moral choice.

The poems that he wrote in the 1930's stressed the tragedy of unemployment, and presented melancholy pictures of 'harvests rotting in the valleys' and 'furnaces gasping in the impossible air'; the worst of these early poems now seem badly dated, but the best have a more durable vitality. A number of them describe, in a kind of nightmare, the bare dramatic fells of northern England (where he spent his holidays as a boy) and the abandoned lead mines left behind by the Romans and the Industrial Revolution. Poems such as 'The Quarry' effectively express the fear of concentration camps or an approaching world war that darkened the 'low dishonest decade' of the 1930's.

Others, less consistently successful, confront us with melodramatic premonitions of vague doom. In a modern ice age the becks turn to glaciers, the fires of the foundries go out, and the Witnesses warn us (rather vaguely) that:

> *Something is going to fall like rain*
> *And it won't be flowers.*

But other poems of this period, especially 'A Summer Night' (1933) or 'Birthday Poem', comment in a striking way on events of sociological importance; they form a lively commentary on contemporary life which succeeds in being chatty and eloquent at the same time.

It is easy to stress Auden's versatility by going on listing the various types of poem that he wrote in the 1930's. There is some excellent occasional literary criticism scattered through these poems, as in the sonnet on Housman; yet another group of poems such as 'Fish in the unruffled Lakes' and 'Our Hunting Fathers' question man's assumption that he is superior to the animals. Another type such as 'Who's Who' shows his mastery of a cryptic type of sonnet. In poems such as 'Song for St. Cecilia's Day' he kept to rhythms that would suit the music of Britten and other composers. He sometimes imitated Anglo-Saxon alliterative verse to express a Nordic fatalism:

> *Doom is dark and deeper than any sea-dingle.*

More often he deliberately used jazz rhythms and the trite, flat language of popular songs; sometimes his purpose in doing this was serious and he pretended to be amused in order to show that he was deeply shocked. But at other times, as in 'Stop all the clocks' (Funeral Blues) it was impossible to tell how serious he intended to be.

The faults of this poetry are a boyish resolve to use images from modern life at all costs, a malicious enjoyment in creating a feeling of impending doom without having any clear idea of its nature, an erratic oscillation between frivolity and sermonising, and, finally, an avoidable obscurity. He caught from Eliot the belief that the

modern poet can defy syntax, can omit necessary connect-
ing words such as 'who' or 'they', and can compel his
reader's intellect to leap gymnastically from one image to
the next. But his virtues are more important than his faults.
He has a gift of arresting phrases such as

> *The slow fastidious line*
> *That disciplines the fell*

or

> *These years have seen a boom in sorrow.*

He is an all-embracing poet who writes with gusto about
every feature of modern life, and has something fresh to say
about each one.

Auden's poetry was much admired in the 1930's by
readers who exaggerated the extent to which it expressed
their own left-wing political views. They tended to find in
Auden what they expected to find. His experience in Spain
had an effect on him that surprised his admirers. He had
been thinking deeply about the failure of liberal humanism
to prevent the Germans, one of the most highly educated
nations in Europe, from adopting the Nazi view that only
effeminate weaklings loved their neighbours as themselves.
He was coming to the conclusion that only Christianity
could invalidate Nazi values. In this mood he had an
important experience at Barcelona during the Civil War.

On arriving in Barcelona, I found as I walked through
the city that all the churches were closed and there was
not a priest to be seen. To my astonishment, this
discovery left me profoundly shocked and disturbed.
The feeling was far too intense to be the result of a mere
liberal dislike of intolerance, the notion that it is wrong
to stop people from doing what they like, even if it is
something silly like going to church. I could not escape
acknowledging that, however I had consciously ignored
and rejected the Church for sixteen years, the existence

of churches and what went on in them had all the time been very important to me.

(from Auden's untitled essay in *Modern Canterbury Pilgrims*, ed. James A. Pike, N.Y., 1956)

At the same time the failure of European democrats to achieve successful political action over Spain convinced him that the dilemma of modern man was too great for a political solution to be enough; his serious interest in psychology and morality convinced him that the Christian solution was more revolutionary and practical than the Marxist one. Indeed it is easy to exaggerate his change of heart; from about 1927 to 1939 his consciously Christian beliefs disappeared underground, only to reappear later — like the streams in the limestone landscape of northern England that meant so much to him.

For some years after he emigrated he held various lectureships in American universities, and in 1946 he became an American citizen; but he half closed the breach with Europe, for he held the elective post of Professor of Poetry at Oxford from 1956 to 1961, and from 1948 he lived partly in New York, partly in Austria. During these later years he attempted an extraordinary range of new ventures. He wrote Christian oratorios for Britten and the libretto of *The Rake's Progress* for Stravinsky; he wrote long religious poems such as *For the Time Being*; and in 1960 he shocked pompous critics by including in *Homage to Clio* a section of facetious light verse.

After his conversion to Christianity he republished many of his poems with important alterations, which have been studied in detail by Joseph Warren Beach in *the Making of the Auden Canon*. His two motives are difficult to separate, for the Marxist phrases that he wished to remove because they expressed ideas that he had discarded were just the phrases whose brash didacticism offended his mature good taste.

The poems of his American middle age are different

from those of his enthusiastic English youth, but they are still very varied and arresting. The fundamental unity of his career as a poet is well expressed by Spender: *His later work is distinguished from his earlier by the attempt to find answers to what, in the earlier, he is content to state as tremendous questions.* But this unity of purpose does not prevent him from alluding to a wide range of human activities — literary, historical, political and cultural — or from using an ingenious variety of verse-forms. It is not true to say, as his critics aver, that respectability quite took the wind out of his sails, or that he was like Wordsworth in abandoning the revolutionary views of his youth to write dull sonnets in his middle age. For Auden continued to write memorable, intelligent and moving verse that illuminates the major problems of our time and shows in an absorbing, but not always serious, way how they present themselves to a witty, lively personality who is interested in an extraordinary range of subjects. As Monroe K. Spears says, he was — *A religious poet who is also a clown, a virtuoso who is incorrigibly didactic, a satirist who is also a musician and a lyricist.*

It may be that his separation from some of the influences that subtly enriched his early poetry — such as the hilly scenery of Northern England — sometimes robbed his later poetry of its vivid and concrete images. But Auden remained an inventive and vital poet. One cannot say that America had made a 'fossil' of him in the way that the Isle of Wight made one of Tennyson. His passionate involvement in the political and religious causes that he championed gives his writing about them a genuine poetic quality, with the result that he is simultaneously intellectual and emotional, witty and sincere; while technically, he was signally successful in fitting the most natural modern language into a great variety of traditional stanza-forms and rhythms.

In 1956 he was elected for a five-year term as Oxford's Professor of Poetry. In 1972 he returned to Christ Church College, Oxford. However he died very suddenly in 1973 when he visited Vienna to give a lecture there.

MISSING

From scars where kestrels hover,
The leader looking over
Into the happy valley,
Orchard and curving river,
May turn away to see
The slow fastidious line
That disciplines the fell,
Hear curlew's creaking call
From angles unforeseen,
The drumming of a snipe   10
Surprise where driven sleet
Had scalded to the bone
And streams are acrid yet
To an unaccustomed lip;
The tall unwounded leader
Of doomed companions, all
Whose voices in the rock
Are now perpetual,
Fighters for no one's sake,
Who died beyond the border.   20
Heroes are buried who
Did not believe in death
And bravery is now
Not in the dying breath
But resisting the temptations
To skyline operations.
Yet glory is not new;
The summer visitors
Still come from far and wide,
Choosing their spots to view   30
The prize competitors,
Each thinking that he will
Find heroes in the wood,
Far from the capital

Where lights and wine are set
For supper by the lake,
But leaders must migrate:
'Leave for Cape Wrath tonight,'
And the host after waiting
Must quench the lamps and pass   40
Alive into the house.

FISH IN THE UNRUFFLED LAKES

FISH in the unruffled lakes
The swarming colours wear,
Swans in the winter air
A white perfection have,
And the great lion walks
Through his innocent grove;
Lion, fish, and swan
Act, and are gone
Upon Time's toppling wave.

We till shadowed days are done,   10
We must weep and sing
Duty's conscious wrong,
The Devil in the clock,
The Goodness carefully worn
For atonement or for luck;
We must lose our loves,
On each beast and bird that moves
Turn an envious look.

Sighs for folly said and done
Twist our narrow days;   20
But I must bless, I must praise
That you, my swan, who have
All gifts that to the swan
Impulsive Nature gave,

The majesty and pride,
Last night should add
Your voluntary love.

THE QUARRY

O WHAT is that sound which so thrills the ear
  Down in the valley drumming, drumming?
Only the scarlet soldiers, dear,
  The soldiers coming.

O what is that light I see flashing so clear
  Over the distance brightly, brightly?
Only the sun on their weapons, dear,
  As they step lightly.

O what are they doing with all that gear,
  What are they doing this morning, this morning?   10
Only their usual manoeuvres, dear,
  Or perhaps a warning.

O why have they left the road down there,
  Why are they suddenly wheeling, wheeling?
Perhaps a change in their orders, dear.
  Why are you kneeling?

O haven't they stopped for the doctor's care,
  Haven't they reined their horses, their horses?
Why, they are none of them wounded, dear,
  None of these forces.   20

O is it the parson they want, with white hair,
  Is it the parson, is it, is it?
No, they are passing his gateway, dear,
  Without a visit.

O it must be the farmer who lives so near.
  It must be the farmer so cunning, so cunning?
They have passed the farmyard already, dear,
  And now they are running.

O where are you going? Stay with me here!
  Were the vows you swore deceiving, deceiving?   30
No, I promised to love you, dear,
  But I must be leaving.

O it's broken the lock and splintered the door,
  O it's the gate where they're turning, turning:
Their boots are heavy on the floor
  And their eyes are burning.

REFUGEE BLUES

SAY this city has ten million souls,
Some are living in mansions, some are living in holes:
Yet there's no place for us, my dear, yet there's no place
    for us.

Once we had a country and we thought it fair,
Look in the atlas and you'll find it there:
We cannot go there now, my dear, we cannot go there
    now.

In the village churchyard there grows an old yew,
Every Spring it blossoms anew:
Old passports can't do that, my dear, old passports can't
    do that.

The consul banged the table and said: 10
'If you've got no passport you're officially dead';
But we are still alive, my dear, but we are still alive.

Went to a committee; they offered me a chair;
Asked me politely to return next year:
But where shall we go to-day, my dear, but where shall
    we go today?

Came to a public meeting, the speaker got up and said:
'If we let them in, they will steal our daily bread';
He was talking of you and me, my dear, he was talking
    of you and me.

Thought I heard the thunder rumbling in the sky;
It was Hitler over Europe, saying: 'They must die';   20
O we were in his mind, my dear, O we were in his mind.

Saw a poodle in a jacket fastened with a pin,
Saw a door opened and a cat let in:
But they weren't German Jews, my dear, but they
    weren't German Jews.

Went down the harbour and stood upon the quay,
Saw the fish swimming as if they were free:
Only ten feet away, my dear, only ten feet away.

Walked through a wood, saw the birds in the trees;
They had no politicians and sang at their ease:
They weren't the human race, my dear, they weren't
    the human race.   30

Dreamed I saw a building with a thousand floors,
A thousand windows and a thousand doors;
Not one of them was ours, my dear, not one of them was
    ours.

Stood on a great plain in the falling snow;
Ten thousand soldiers marched to and fro:
Looking for you and me, my dear, looking for you and
    me.

LAY YOUR SLEEPING HEAD, MY LOVE

LAY your sleeping head, my love,
Human on my faithless arm;
Time and fevers burn away
Individual beauty from
Thoughtful children, and the grave
Proves the child ephemeral:
But in my arms till break of day
Let the living creature lie,
Mortal, guilty, but to me
The entirely beautiful.   10

Soul and body have no bounds:
To lovers as they lie upon
Her tolerant enchanted slope
In their ordinary swoon,
Grave the vision Venus sends
Of supernatural sympathy,
Universal love and hope;
While an abstract insight wakes
Among the glaciers and the rocks
The hermit's sensual ecstasy.   20

Certainty, fidelity
On the stroke of midnight pass
Like vibrations of a bell,
And fashionable madmen raise
Their pedantic boring cry:
Every farthing of the cost,
All the dreadful cards foretell,
Shall be paid, but from this night
Not a whisper, not a thought,
Not a kiss nor look be lost.   30

Beauty, midnight, vision dies:
Let the winds of dawn that blow
Softly round your dreaming head
Such a day of sweetness show
Eye and knocking heart may bless,
Find the mortal world enough;
Noons of dryness see you fed
By the involuntary powers,
Nights of insult let you pass
Watched by every human love.   40

BIRTHDAY POEM
(*To Christopher Isherwood*)

AUGUST for the people and their favourite islands.
Daily the steamers sidle up to meet
The effusive welcome of the pier, and soon
The luxuriant life of the steep stone valleys,
The sallow oval faces of the city
Begot in passion or good-natured habit,
Are caught by waiting coaches, or laid bare
Beside the undiscriminating sea.

Lulled by the light they live their dreams of freedom;
May climb the old road twisting to the moors,   10
Play leap frog, enter cafés, wear
The tigerish blazer and the dove-like shoe.
The yachts upon the little lake are theirs,
The gulls ask for them, and to them the band
Makes its tremendous statements; they control
The complicated apparatus of amusement.

All types that can intrigue the writer's fancy,
Or sensuality approves, are here.
And I, each meal-time with the families,
The animal brother and his serious sister,   20

Or after breakfast on the urned steps watching
The defeated and disfigured marching by,
Have thought of you, Christopher, and wished beside me
Your squat spruce body and enormous head.

Nine years ago, upon that southern island
Where the wild Tennyson became a fossil,
Half-boys, we spoke of books and praised
The acid and austere, behind us only
The stuccoed suburb and expensive school.
Scented the turf, the distant baying   30
Nice decoration to the artist's wish;
Yet fast the deer were flying through the wood.

Our hopes were set still on the spies' career,
Prizing the glasses and the old felt hat,
And all the secrets we discovered were
Extraordinary and false; for this one coughed
And it was gasworks coke, and that one laughed
And it was snow in bedrooms; many wore wigs,
The coastguard signalled messages of love,
The enemy were sighted from the Norman tower.   40

Five summers pass and now we watch
The Baltic from a balcony: the word is love.
Surely one fearless kiss would cure
The million fevers, a stroking brush
The insensitive refuse from the burning core.
Was there a dragon who had closed the works
While the starved city fed it with the Jews?
Then love would train it with his trainer's look.

Pardon the studied taste that could refuse
The golf-house quick one and the rector's tea;   50
Pardon the nerves the thrushes could not soothe,
Yet answered promptly the no-subtler lure
To private joking in a panelled room,
The solitary vitality of tramps and madmen;

Believed the whisper in the double bed:
Pardon for these and every flabby fancy.

For now the moulding images of growth
That made our interest and us, are gone.
Louder to-day the wireless roars
Warnings and lies, and it is little comfort   60
Among the well-shaped cosily to flit,
Or longer to desire about our lives
The beautiful loneliness of the banks, or find
The stoves and resignations of the frozen plains.

The close-set eyes of mother's boy
Saw nothing to be done; we look up again:
See Scandal praying with her sharp knees up,
And Virtue stood at Weeping Cross,
The green thumb to the ledger knuckled down,
And Courage to his leaking ship appointed,   70
Slim Truth dismissed without a character,
And gaga Falsehood highly recommended.

Greed showing shamelessly her naked money,
And all Love's wondering eloquence debased
To a collector's slang, Smartness in furs,
And Beauty scratching miserably for food,
Honour self-sacrificed for Calculation,
And Reason stoned by Mediocrity,
Freedom by Power shockingly maltreated,
And Justice exiled till Saint Geoffrey's Day.   80

So in this hour of crisis and dismay,
What better than your strict and adult pen
Can warn us from the colours and the consolations,
The showy arid works, reveal
The squalid shadow of academy and garden,
Make action urgent and its nature clear?
Who give us nearer insight to resist
The expanding fear, the savaging disaster?

This then my birthday wish for you, as now
From the narrow window of my fourth floor room   90
I smoke into the night, and watch reflections
Stretch in the harbour. In the houses
The little pianos are closed, and a clock strikes.
And all sway forward on the dangerous flood
Of history, that never sleeps or dies,
And, held one moment, burns the hand.

1st SEPTEMBER 1939

I sit in one of the dives
On Fifty-Second Street
Uncertain and afraid
As the clever hopes expire
Of a low dishonest decade:
Waves of anger and fear
Circulate over the bright
And darkened lands of the earth,
Obsessing our private lives;
The unmentionable odour of death   10
Offends the September night.

Accurate scholarship can
Unearth the whole offence
From Luther until now
That has driven a culture mad,
Find what occurred at Linz,
What huge imago made
A psychopathic god:
I and the public know
What all schoolchildren learn,   20
Those to whom evil is done
Do evil in return.

Exiled Thucydides knew
All that a speech can say
About Democracy,
And what dictators do,
The elderly rubbish they talk
To an apathetic grave;
Analysed all in his book,
The enlightenment driven away,   30
The habit-forming pain,
Mismanagement and grief:
We must suffer them all again.

Into this neutral air
Where blind skyscrapers use
Their full height to proclaim
The strength of Collective Man,
Each language pours its vain
Competitive excuse:
But who can live for long   40
In an euphoric dream;
Out of the mirror they stare,
Imperialism's face
And the international wrong.

Faces along the bar
Cling to their average day:
The lights must never go out,
The music must always play,
All the conventions conspire
To make this fort assume   50
The furniture of home;
Lest we should see where we are,
Lost in a haunted wood,
Children afraid of the night
Who have never been happy or good.

The windiest militant trash
Important Persons shout

Is not so crude as our wish:
What mad Nijinsky wrote
About Diaghilev   60
Is true of the normal heart;
For the error bred in the bone
Of each woman and each man
Craves what it cannot have,
Not universal love
But to be loved alone.

From the conservative dark
Into the ethical life
The dense commuters come,
Repeating their morning vow;   70
'I *will* be true to the wife,
I'll concentrate more on my work,'
And helpless governors wake
To resume their compulsory game:
Who can release them now,
Who can reach the deaf,
Who can speak for the dumb?

Defenceless under the night
Our world in stupor lies;
Yet, dotted everywhere,   80
Ironic points of light
Flash out wherever the Just
Exchange their messages:
May I, composed like them
Of Eros and of dust,
Beleaguered by the same
Negation and despair,
Show an affirming flame.

THE UNKNOWN CITIZEN
(To JS/07/M/378
This Marble Monument
Is Erected by the State)

HE was found by the Bureau of Statistics to be
One against whom there was no official complaint,
And all the reports on his conduct agree
That, in the modern sense of an old-fashioned word, he
    was a saint,
For in everything he did he served the Great Community.
Except for the War till the day he retired
He worked in a factory and never got fired,
But satisfied his employers, Fudge Motors Inc.
Yet he wasn't a scab or odd in his views,
For his Union reports that he paid his dues,   10
(Our report on his Union shows it was sound)
And our Social Psychology workers found
That he was popular with his mates and liked a drink.
The Press are convinced that he bought a paper every
    day
And that his reactions to advertisements were normal in
    every way.
Policies taken out in his name prove that he was fully
    insured,
And his Health-card shows he was once in hospital but
    left it cured.
Both Producers Research and High-Grade Living declare
He was fully sensible to the advantages of the Instalment
    Plan
And had everything necessary to the Modern Man,   20
A phonograph, a radio, a car and a frigidaire.
Our researchers into Public Opinion are content
That he held the proper opinions for the time of year;
When there was peace, he was for peace; when there was
    war, he went.

He was married and added five children to the
    population,
Which our Eugenist says was the right number for a
    parent of his generation,
And our teachers report that he never interfered with
    their education.
Was he free? Was he happy? The question is absurd:
Had anything been wrong, we should certainly have
    heard.

THE MANAGERS

IN the bad old days, it was not so bad:
    The top of the ladder
Was an amusing place to sit; success
    Meant quite a lot — leisure
And huge meals, more palaces filled with more
    Objects, books, girls, horses
Than one would ever get round to, and to be
    Carried uphill while seeing
Others walk. To rule was a pleasure when
    One wrote a death-sentence   10
On the back of the Ace of Spades and played on
    With a new deck. Honours
Are not so physical or jolly now,
    For the species of Powers
We are used to are not like that. Could one of them
    Be said to resemble
The Tragic Hero, the Platonic Saint,
    Or would any painter
Portray one rising triumphant from a lake
    On a dolphin, naked,   20
Protected by an umbrella of cherubs? Can
    They so much as manage
To behave like genuine Caesars when alone
    Or drinking with cronies,

To let their hair down and be frank about
    The world? It is doubtful.
The last word on how we may live or die
    Rests to-day with such quiet
Men, working too hard in rooms that are too big,
    Reducing to figures   30
What is the matter, what is to be done.
    A neat little luncheon
Of sandwiches is brought to each on a tray,
    Nourishment they are able
To take with one hand without looking up
    From papers a couple
Of secretaries are needed to file,
    From problems no smiling
Can dismiss: the typewriters never stop
    But whirr like grasshoppers   40
In the silent siesta heat as, frivolous
    Across their discussions,
From woods unaltered by our wars and our vows
    There drift the scents of flowers
And the song of birds who will never vote
    Or bother to notice
Those distinguishing marks a lover sees
    By instinct and policemen
Can be trained to observe; far into the night
    Their windows burn brightly   50
And, behind their backs bent over some report,
    On every quarter,
For ever like a god or a disease
    There on the earth the reason
In all its aspects why they are tired, the weak,
    The inattentive, seeking
Someone to blame; if, to recuperate
    They go a-playing, their greatness
Encounters the bow of the chef or the glance
    Of the ballet-dancer   60
Who cannot be ruined by any master's fall.
    To rule must be a calling,

It seems, like surgery or sculpture, the fun
   Neither love nor money
But taking necessary risks, the test
   Of one's skill, the question,
If difficult, their own reward. But then
   Perhaps one should mention
Also what must be a comfort as they guess
   In times like the present   70
When guesses can prove so fatally wrong,
   The fact of belonging
To the very select indeed, to those
   For whom, just supposing
They do, there will be places on the last
   Plane out of disaster.
No: no one is really sorry for their
   Heavy gait and careworn
Look, nor would they thank you if you said you were.

EMBASSY

As evening fell the day's oppression lifted;
Far peaks came into focus; it had rained:
Across wide lawns and cultured flowers drifted
The conversation of the highly trained.

Two gardeners watched them pass and priced their shoes:
A chauffeur waited, reading in the drive,
For them to finish their exchange of views;
It seemed a picture of the private life.

Far off, no matter what good they intended,
The armies waited for a verbal error   10
With all the instruments for causing pain:

And on the issue of their charm depended
A land laid waste, with all its young men slain,
Its women weeping, and its towns in terror.

THE SHIELD OF ACHILLES

    SHE looked over his shoulder
        For vines and olive trees,
    Marble well-governed cities
        And ships upon untamed seas,
    But there on the shining metal
        His hands had put instead
    An artificial wilderness
        And a sky like lead.

A plain without a feature, bare and brown,
    No blade of grass, no sign of neighbourhood,   10
Nothing to eat and nowhere to sit down,
    Yet, congregated on its blankness, stood
    An unintelligible multitude.
A million eyes, a million boots in line,
Without expression, waiting for a sign.

Out of the air a voice without a face
    Proved by statistics that some cause was just
In tones as dry and level as the place:
    No one was cheered and nothing was discussed;
    Column by column in a cloud of dust   20
They marched away enduring a belief
Whose logic brought them, somewhere else, to grief.

    She looked over his shoulder
        For ritual pieties,
    White flower-garlanded heifers,
        Libation and sacrifice,
    But there on the shining metal

> Where the altar should have been,
> She saw by his flickering forge-light
>   Quite another scene.   30

Barbed wire enclosed an arbitrary spot
    Where bored officials lounged (one cracked a joke)
And sentries sweated for the day was hot:
    A crowd of ordinary decent folk
    Watched from without and neither moved nor spoke
As three pale figures were led forth and bound
To three posts driven upright in the ground.

The mass and majesty of this world, all
    That carries weight and always weighs the same
Lay in the hands of others; they were small   40
    And could not hope for help and no help came:
    What their foes liked to do was done, their shame
Was all the worst could wish; they lost their pride
And died as men before their bodies died.

> She looked over his shoulder
>   For athletes at their games,
> Men and women in a dance
>   Moving their sweet limbs
> Quick, quick, to music,
>   But there on the shining shield   50
> His hands had set no dancing-floor
>   But a weed-choked field.

A ragged urchin, aimless and alone,
    Loitered about that vacancy, a bird
Flew up to safety from his well-aimed stone:
    That girls are raped, that two boys knife a third,
    Were axioms to him, who'd never heard
Of any world where promises were kept.
Or one could weep because another wept.

The thin-lipped armourer,
   Hephaestos hobbled away,
Thetis of the shining breasts
   Cried out in dismay
At what the god had wrought
   To please her son, the strong
Iron-hearted man-slaying Achilles
   Who would not live long.

IN PRAISE OF LIMESTONE

IF it form the one landscape that we the inconstant ones
   Are consistently homesick for, this is chiefly
Because it dissolves in water. Mark these rounded slopes
   With their surface fragrance of thyme and beneath
A secret system of caves and conduits; hear these springs
   That spurt out everywhere with a chuckle
Each filling a private pool for its fish and carving
   Its own little ravine whose cliffs entertain
The butterfly and the lizard; examine this region
   Of short distances and definite places: 10
What could be more like Mother or a fitter background
   For her son, the flirtatious male who lounges
Against a rock in the sunlight, never doubting
   That for all his faults he is loved, whose works are but
Extensions of his power to charm? From weathered
      outcrop
   To hill-top temple, from appearing waters to
Conspicuous fountains, from a wild to a formal vineyard,
   Are ingenious but short steps that a child's wish
To receive more attention than his brothers, whether
   By pleasing or teasing, can easily take.   20

Watch, then, the band of rivals as they climb up and
      down

Their steep stone gennels in twos and threes,
   sometimes
Arm in arm, but never, thank God, in step; or engaged
   On the shady side of a square at midday in
Voluble discourse, knowing each other too well to think
   There are any important secrets, unable
To conceive a god whose temper-tantrums are moral
   And not to be pacified by a clever line
Or a good lay: for, accustomed to a stone that responds,
   They have never had to veil their faces in awe   30
Of a crater whose blazing fury could not be fixed;
   Adjusted to the local needs of valleys
Where everything can be touched or reached by walking,
   Their eyes have never looked into infinite space
Through the lattice-work of a nomad's comb; born
     lucky,
   Their legs have never encountered the fungi
And insects of the jungle, the monstrous forms and lives
   With which we have nothing, we like to hope, in
     common.
So, when one of them goes to the bad, the way his mind
     works
   Remains comprehensible: to become a pimp   40
Or deal in fake jewellery or ruin a fine tenor voice
   For effects that bring down the house could happen
     to all
But the best and the worst of us . . .
                    That is why, I suppose,
   The best and worst never stayed here long but sought
Immoderate soils where the beauty was not so external,
   The light less public and the meaning of life
Something more than a mad camp. 'Come!' cried the
     granite wastes,
   'How evasive is your humour, how accidental
Your kindest kiss, how permanent is death.' (Saints-to-be
   Slipped away sighing.) 'Come!' purred the clays and
     gravels.   50
'On our plains there is room for armies to drill; rivers

Wait to be tamed and slaves to construct you a tomb
In the grand manner: soft as the earth is mankind and
     both
     Need to be altered.' (Intendant Caesars rose and
Left, slamming the door.) But the really reckless were
     fetched
     By an older colder voice, the oceanic whisper:
'I am the solitude that asks and promises nothing;
     That is how I shall set you free. There is no love;
There are only the various envies, all of them sad.'

They were right, my dear, all those voices were right   60
And still are; this land is not the sweet home that it
     looks,
     Nor its peace the historical calm of a site
Where something was settled once and for all: A
     backward
     And dilapidated province, connected
To the big busy world by a tunnel, with a certain
     Seedy appeal, is that all it is now? Not quite:
It has a worldly duty which in spite of itself
     It does not neglect, but calls into question
All the Great Powers assume; it disturbs our rights. The
     poet,
     Admired for his earnest habit of calling   70
The sun the sun, his mind Puzzle, is made uneasy
     By these solid statutes which so obviously doubt
His antimythological myth; and these gamins,
     Pursuing the scientist down the tiled colonnade
With such lively offers, rebuke his concern for Nature's
     Remotest aspects: I, too, am reproached, for what
And how much you know. Not to lose time, not to get
     caught,
     Not to be left behind, not, please! to resemble
The beasts who repeat themselves, or a thing like water
     Or stone whose conduct can be predicted, these   80
Are our Common Prayer, whose greatest comfort is music
     Which can be made anywhere, is invisible,

And does not smell. In so far as we have to look forward
    To death as a fact, no doubt we are right: but if
Sins can be forgiven, if bodies rise from the dead,
    These modifications of matter into
Innocent athletes and gesticulating fountains,
    Made solely for pleasure, make a further point:
The blessed will not care what angle they are regarded
      from,
    Having nothing to hide. Dear, I know nothing of   90
Either, but when I try to imagine a faultless love
    Or the life to come, what I hear is the murmur
Of underground streams, what I see is a limestone
      landscape.

R. S. THOMAS

FOR over a century after Wordsworth and Coleridge published *Lyrical Ballads* many English poets were more interested in the country than in the town, and tended to agree with Wordsworth that:

> *One impulse from a vernal wood*
> *Can teach you more of man,*
> *Of moral evil and of good,*
> *Than all the sages can.*

The Georgians, the last generation of poets of this period, concentrated on the pleasanter aspects of the countryside, and seemed to be out of touch with the contemporary world now that most people lived in towns. Critics reacted against them and argued that Hardy was the last poet who could be forgiven for writing so much about rural life because he had undisputably been brought up in the midst of it, and because he wrote honestly about its tragedies as well as its beauties. There have, however, been poets in this century who have lived in the country, have made themselves an integral part of the rural life and community around them, and have developed new styles to express their individual, sincere and up-to-date impressions of the country as it really is today. For some readers this is the world that they still live in, and for town-dwellers too this is a world that they frequently visit and need poets to interpret.

R. S. Thomas is an interesting example of a poet who has stubbornly ignored critics' assumptions that modern poetry must be urban. Though born in semi-anglicised Cardiff in 1913, he has spent most of his life as a country parson among the Welsh-speaking hill farmers of Powys and Gwynedd in Central Wales. He has an appreciative eye for natural beauty, urging us to notice it

and treasure it in our memory as one remembers in winter
the last beautiful windless day in autumn, but he is more
interested in country people than in country scenes, and
the part of Wales that he writes about is harsh as well as
beautiful. Mid-Wales seems attractive to the English
tourist who speeds along its few river valleys in a comfortable car on his way to Aberystwyth; and it is pleasant to
gaze at its crab-apple trees in blossom on a May morning
or its long village streets enjoying the tranquil sunshine of
an August afternoon; but the valleys are steep and narrow,
and their wind-swept sides rise quickly to a wilderness of
bracken and heather, broken up by outcrops of rock,
isolated farmhouses built of rough-hewn slate blocks, and
the ruins of feudal fortresses (for you cannot forget the
past — *at least not in Wales*).

It is not easy to make a living in this area, and the
population is persistently declining. The *mouldering quarries
and mines* remind us that the whole world bought vast
quantities of Welsh slate before 1914 but does so no longer,
while roads are no longer built to the Welsh lead and gold
mines as they were by the Romans. The typical inhabitant
is a small hill-farmer keeping sheep on the infertile
mountainsides and growing a few kale or mangolds in an
occasional field that is more sheltered than most. At a
certain height above sea-level the trees come to an end, as
Thomas reminds us when he describes climbing up a rough
track to reach an isolated farm where a peasant woman
has *lasted* till her ninetieth birthday. In 'A Welsh Testa-
ment' Thomas seems to upbraid English voters for wanting
to keep most of Wales a sort of national park without *the
loud roar of hot tractors*, instead of paying for research into
better types of grass that will grow at over 1,000 feet,
or taking other steps to help the hill-farmer.

There will always be a stern limit to how far the farmers
of mid-Wales can overcome the disadvantages of their
locality. It is one of the wettest parts of Britain, and on
many days the clouds come down low over the mountains,
so that the farmhouses are *huddled between grey walls of cloud*

for at least half the year. In March, or even sometimes May, the snow still lingers on the mountain-tops, and on lovely October afternoons Thomas seems to shiver at the thought of 'the long cold' ahead of him.

Thomas's chief interest is in the people who struggle to make a living in these small villages and lonely farms. As he gets to know them better he learns from them how to accept life philosophically; they are, he insists, 'the dark well' from which he draws up his awareness of the poetry of life. They are also a source from which he learns more about God, for he seems to see a close connection between religion and effort, and he draws closer to God as he watches the effort of a great violinist or a humble peasant. He learned Welsh as an adult in order to talk to his parishioners in their own language and so to get to know them better; his impressions of them as he visits them provide the starting points for his poems. His attitude to them is an ambivalent one, for he sees their faults and their virtues with equal clarity. He urges his readers to feel sympathy for unambitious farmers *stumbling insensitively from furrow to furrow*, though their *education or class or creed* is so different from that of the typical inhabitant of London — or Cardiff. But he admits the faults or uncouthness of these farmers, such as their *stinking garments* or their *aimless grin*. He invites us to see the genuine emotions and hopes hidden beneath the unattractive exterior. He admires their characters as much as Wordsworth admired the Leech-gatherer or Michael, though he presents their faults more realistically. For his language and his rhythm are un-flinchingly modern in their candour and their flexibility, and he manages to write about country people as though he had never read a line of Wordsworth.

WELSH LANDSCAPE

To live in Wales is to be conscious
At dusk of the spilled blood
That went to the making of the wild sky,
Dyeing the immaculate rivers
In all their courses.
It is to be aware,
Above the noisy tractor
And hum of the machine
Of strife in the strung woods,
Vibrant with sped arrows.   10
You cannot live in the present,
At least not in Wales.
There is the language for instance,
The soft consonants
Strange to the ear.
There are cries in the dark at night
As owls answer the moon,
And thick ambush of shadows,
Hushed at the fields' corners
There is no present in Wales,   20
And no future;
There is only the past,
Brittle with relics,
Wind-bitten towers and castles
With sham ghosts;
Mouldering quarries and mines;
And an impotent people,
Sick with inbreeding,
Worrying the carcase of an old song.

A WELSH TESTAMENT

ALL right, I was Welsh. Does it matter?
I spoke the tongue that was passed on
To me in the place I happened to be,
A place huddled between grey walls
Of cloud for at least half the year.
My word for heaven was not yours.
The word for hell had a sharp edge
Put on it by the hand of the wind
Honing, honing with a shrill sound
Day and night. Nothing that Glyn Dŵr   10
Knew was armour against the rain's
Missiles. What was descent from him?

Even God had a Welsh name:
We spoke to him in the old language;
He was to have a peculiar care
For the Welsh people. History showed us
He was too big to be nailed to the wall
Of a stone chapel, yet still we crammed him
Between the boards of a black book.

Yet men sought us despite this.   20
My high cheek-bones, my length of skull
Drew them as to a rare portrait
By a dead master. I saw them stare
From their long cars, as I passed knee-deep
In ewes and wethers. I saw them stand
By the thorn hedges, watching me string
The far flocks on a shrill whistle.

And always there was their eyes' strong
Pressure on me; You are Welsh, they said;
Speak to us so; keep your fields free   30
Of the smell of petrol, the loud roar

Of hot tractors; we must have peace
And quietness.
                    Is a museum
Peace? I asked. Am I the keeper
Of the heart's relics, blowing the dust
In my own eyes? I am a man;
I never wanted the drab role
Life assigned me, an actor playing
To the past's audience upon a stage
Of earth and stone; the absurd label   40
Of birth, of race hanging askew
About my shoulders. I was in prison
Until you came; your voice was a key
Turning in the enormous lock
Of hopelessness. Did the door open
To let me out or yourselves in?

AFFINITY

CONSIDER this man in the field beneath,
Gaitered with mud, lost in his own breath,
Without joy, without sorrow,
Without children, without wife,
Stumbling insensitively from furrow to furrow,
A vague somnambulist; but hold your tears
For his name also is written in the Book of Life.

Ransack your brainbox, pull out the drawers
That rot in your heart's dust, and what have you to give
To enrich his spirit or the way he lives?   10
From the standpoint of education or caste or creed
Is there anything to show that your essential need
Is less than his, who has the world for church,
And stands bare-headed in the woods' wide porch
Morning and evening to hear God's choir
Scatter their praises? Don't be taken in

By stinking garments or an aimless grin;
He also is human, and the same small star,
That lights you homeward, has inflamed his mind
With the old hunger, born of his kind.   20

DEATH OF A PEASANT

You remember Davies? He died, you know,
With his face to the wall, as the manner is
Of the poor peasant in his stone croft
On the Welsh hills. I recall the room
Under the slates, and the smirched snow
Of the wide bed in which he lay,
Lonely as an ewe that is sick to lamb
In the hard weather of mid-March.
I remember also the trapped wind
Tearing the curtains, and the wild light's   10
Frequent hysteria upon the floor,
The bare floor without a rug
Or mat to soften the loud tread
Of neighbours crossing the uneasy boards
To peer at Davies with gruff words
Of meaningless comfort, before they turned
Heartless away from the stale smell
Of death in league with those dank walls.

SOIL

A FIELD with tall hedges and a young
Moon in the branches and one star
Declining westward set the scene
Where he works slowly astride the rows
Of red mangolds and green swedes
Plying mechanically his cold blade.

This is his world, the hedge defines
The mind's limits; only the sky
Is boundless, and he never looks up;
His gaze is deep in the dark soil,   10
As are his feet. The soil is all;
His hands fondle it, and his bones
Are formed out of it with the swedes.
And if sometimes the knife errs,
Burying itself in his shocked flesh,
Then out of the wound the blood seeps home
To the warm soil from which it came.

THE POACHER

TURNING aside, never meeting
In the still lanes, fly infested,
Our frank greeting with quick smile,
You are the wind that set the bramble
Aimlessly clawing the void air.
The fox knows you, the sly weasel
Feels always the steel comb
Of eyes parting like sharp rain
Among the grasses its smooth fur.
No smoke haunting the cold chimney   10
Over your hearth betrays your dwelling
In blue writing above the trees.
The robed night, your dark familiar,
Covers your movements; the slick sun,
A dawn accomplice, removes your tracks
One by one from the bright dew.

THE LABOURER

THERE he goes, tacking against the fields'
Uneasy tides. What have the centuries done
To change him? The same garments, frayed with light
Or seamed with rain, cling to the wind-scoured bones
And shame him in the eyes of the spruce birds.
Once it was ignorance, then need, but now
Habit that drapes him on a bush of cloud
For life to mock at, while the noisy surf
Of people dins far off at the world's rim.
He has been here since life began, a vague   10
Movement among the roots of the young grass.
Bend down and peer beneath the twigs of hair,
And look into the hard eyes, flecked with care;
What do you see? Notice the twitching hands,
Veined like a leaf, and tough bark of the limbs,
Wrinkled and gnarled, and tell me what you think.
A wild tree still, whose seasons are not yours,
The slow heart beating to the hidden pulse
Of the strong sap, the feet firm in the soil?
No, no, a man like you, but blind with tears   20
Of sweat to the bright star that draws you on.

THE DARK WELL

THEY see you as they see you,
A poor farmer with no name,
Ploughing cloudward, sowing the wind
With squalls of gulls at the day's end.
To me you are Prytherch, the man
Who more than all directed my slow
Charity where there was need.

There are two hungers, hunger for bread
And hunger of the uncouth soul
For the light's grace. I have seen both,   10
And chosen for an indulgent world's
Ear the story of one whose hands
Have bruised themselves on the locked doors
Of life; whose heart, fuller than mine
Of gulped tears, is the dark well
From which to draw, drop after drop,
The terrible poetry of his kind.

NINETIETH BIRTHDAY

You go up the long track
That will take a car, but is best walked
On slow foot, noting the lichen
That writes history on the page
Of the grey rock. Trees are about you
At first, but yield to the green bracken,
The nightjar's house: you can hear it spin
On warm evenings; it is still now
In the noonday heat, only the lesser
Voices sound, blue-fly and gnat   10
And the stream's whisper. As the road climbs,
You will pause for breath and the far sea's
Signal will flash, till you turn again
To the steep track, buttressed with cloud.

And there at the top that old woman,
Born almost a century back
In that stone farm, awaits your coming;
Waits for the news of the lost village
She thinks she knows, a place that exists
In her memory only.
                              You bring her greeting   20
And praise for having lasted so long

With time's knife shaving the bone.
Yet no bridge joins her own
World with yours, all you can do
Is lean kindly across the abyss
To hear words that were once wise.

EVANS

Evans? Yes, many a time
I came down his bare flight
Of stairs into the gaunt kitchen
With its wood fire, where crickets sang
Accompaniment to the black kettle's
Whine, and so into the cold
Dark to smother in the thick tide
Of night that drifted about the walls
Of his stark farm on the hill ridge.

It was not the dark filling my eyes   10
And mouth appalled me; not even the drip
Of rain like blood from the one tree
Weather-tortured. It was the dark
Silting the veins of that sick man
I left stranded upon the vast
And lonely shore of his bleak bed.

THE MUSICIAN

A memory of Kreisler once:
At some recital in this same city,
The seats all taken, I found myself pushed
On to the stage with a few others,
So near that I could see the toil
Of his face muscles, a pulse like a moth

Fluttering under the fine skin,
And the indelible veins of his smooth brow.

I could see, too, the twitching of the fingers,
Caught temporarily in art's neurosis,   10
As we sat there or warmly applauded
This player who so beautifully suffered
For each of us upon his instrument.

So it must have been on Calvary
In the fiercer light of the thorns' halo:
The men standing by and that one figure,
The hands bleeding, the mind bruised but calm,
Making such music as lives still.
And no one daring to interrupt
Because it was himself that he played   20
And closer than all of them the God listened.

THE VILLAGE

SCARCELY a street, too few houses
To merit the title; just a way between
The one tavern and the one shop
That leads nowhere and fails at the top
Of the short hill, eaten away
By long erosion of the green tide
Of grass creeping perpetually nearer
This last outpost of time past.

So little happens; the black dog
Cracking his fleas in the hot sun   10
Is history. Yet the girl who crosses
From door to door moves to a scale
Beyond the bland day's two dimensions.

Stay, then, village, for round you spins
On slow axis a world as vast
And meaningful as any poised
By great Plato's solitary mind.

THE VIEW FROM THE WINDOW

LIKE a painting it is set before one,
But less brittle, ageless; these colours
Are renewed daily with variations
Of light and distance that no painter
Achieves or suggests. Then there is movement,
Change, as slowly the cloud bruises
Are healed by sunlight, or snow caps
A black mood; but gold at evening
To cheer the heart. All through history
The great brush has not rested,   10
Nor the paint dried; yet what eye,
Looking coolly, or, as we now,
Through the tears' lenses, ever saw
This work and it was not finished.

AUTUMN ON THE LAND

A MAN, a field, silence — what is there to say?
He lives, he moves, and the October day
Burns slowly down.
                    History is made
Elsewhere; the hours forfeit to time's blade
Don't matter here. The leaves large and small,
Shed by the branches, unlamented fall
About his shoulders. You may look in vain
Through the eyes' window; on his meagre hearth
The thin, shy soul has not begun its reign

Over the darkness. Beauty, love and mirth   10
And joy are strangers there.
                              You must revise
Your bland philosophy of nature, earth
Has of itself no power to make men wise.

A BLACKBIRD SINGING

It seems wrong that out of this bird,
Black, bold, a suggestion of dark
Places about it, there yet should come
Such rich music, as though the notes'
Ore were changed to a rare metal
At one touch of that bright bill.

You have heard it often, alone at your desk
In a green April, your mind drawn
Away from its work by sweet disturbance
Of the mild evening outside your room.   10

A slow singer, but loading each phrase
With history's overtones, love, joy
And grief learned by his dark tribe
In other orchards and passed on
Instinctively as they are now,
But fresh always with new tears.

A DAY IN AUTUMN

It will not always be like this,
The air windless, a few last
Leaves adding their decoration
To the trees' shoulders, braiding the cuffs
Of the boughs with gold; a bird preening

In the lawn's mirror. Having looked up
From the day's chores, pause a minute,
Let the mind take its photograph
Of the bright scene, something to wear
Against the heart in the long cold.   10

DYLAN THOMAS

Dylan Thomas was born in 1914 in Swansea, where his father taught English at the Grammar School. His prose works show us how fascinating a place Swansea was to him as a boy. It still contains, within its municipal boundaries, some of the ugliest and some of the loveliest parts of the British Isles, and when Thomas was young this contrast was even greater. Close to the oldest parts of the town, later to be destroyed by German bombers, was Swansea's pleasant beach, while within walking distance for an active boy were the unspoilt beauties of the Gower Peninsula. Thomas recounts the thrills of his boyhood in his semi-autobiographical short stories, *Portrait of the Artist as a Young Dog*, and in his broadcast talks published under the title of *Quite Early One Morning*. He tells us:

> I was born in a large Welsh industrial town at the beginning of the Great War: an ugly, lovely town (or so it was, and is, to me), crawling, sprawling, slummed, unplanned, jerry-villa'd, and smug-suburbed by the side of a long and splendid-curving shore where truant boys and anonymous old men, in the tatters and hang-overs of a hundred charity suits, beach-combed, idled, and paddled, watched the dock-bound boats, and threw stones into the sea for barking outcast dogs.

When Thomas left school he worked for a year as a reporter on a Swansea newspaper and then risked his chances in London, where he made a precarious living by doing odd jobs for newspapers such as reviewing thrillers. During the Second World War Thomas, who was rejected for the army as medically unfit, won a deserved reputation as a script-writer and broadcaster for the B.B.C. He exerted a magnetic influence on all who listened to his reading of poetry on the radio or on gramophone records.

His warm, powerful voice and his essential sincerity made many poems — either written by himself or by a wide variety of other poets — sound greater than they had ever seemed before. He was also becoming notorious as a bohemian personality who drank too much, was an irresponsible spendthrift, and either amused or shocked his listeners with outrageous witticisms. Whereas Auden's poetry was losing popularity because its political ideas seemed out of date as soon as the war began, Thomas offered poetry-readers what they wanted in the 1940's. His poetry did not argue about politics; instead it was lyrical in a challenging (sometimes enigmatic) manner about sex, religion and death. For ten years or more he was the model whom the young poets copied.

In 1937 he married Caitlin Macnamara, a niece of Augustus John the painter, and they went to live in Laugharne. It is a picturesque little seaside town near to the farm where he had stayed as a boy with his aunt — the farm that is described in 'After the Funeral' and 'Fern Hill'. Laugharne's ruined castle, covered with ivy, looks down on a Lilliputian harbour and a wide, shallow estuary. At low tide the drying sands stretch for miles, but at high tide the dazzle of the sea comes right into the town.

Thomas's death in the U.S.A. in 1953 was hastened — and dramatised — by his three tours of America, during which he delighted huge public audiences with his inspired readings of poetry but shocked many people who met him in private by his reckless drinking and conversation. J. M. Brinnin, the American critic who arranged these tours, has given us a vivid account of them in *Dylan Thomas in America*. A few minutes before a public reading Dylan Thomas would be overwhelmed by violent fits of sickness and coughing. *Yet at the appointed time he walked on to the stage, shoulders straight, chest out in his staunch and pouter-pigeon advance, and proceeded to give . . . those performances which were to bring to America a whole new concept of poetry reading.*

He arrived in America for the last time in October 1953. He looked very ill indeed, but he was able to see the first performance of *Under Milk Wood*, in which the inhabitants of a thinly disguised Laugharne reveal their emotions and daydreams in poetic prose. A few days later he died in hospital of 'direct alcoholic toxicity in brain tissue and brain cells'. Immediately, journalists who had never read a word of his poetry joined with those poets who had read every word of it in raising melodramatic cries of exaggerated grief and adulation. In America admirers collected the money to fly his body back to Laugharne, while in Britain they made assertions as hysterical as George Barker's claim that the death of Thomas represented *the undisguised intervention of the powers of darkness in our affairs*.

The best we can say for Thomas as a man is that he was always honest and sincere, that he was rude only to those people whose interest in poetry seemed to him to be mere pretence, and that he was driven to drink by the fear that he had outlived his inspiration. Certainly, he had written very little in the last seven years of his life.

His poems can be divided into three categories: firstly those that are almost surrealist, secondly those few that are straightforward, and thirdly those that present nostalgic memories of his childhood or regret the deaths of people near to him.

The first category includes most of his poems, especially those that would be classed by his most fervent admirers as representing the true authentic Dylan. Just as Freud believed that if a psychiatrist's patient could be helped to reveal the memories buried in his subconscious, he would be on his way to recover peace of mind, so the Surrealists believed that if the poet dredged up a miscellany of images from his subconscious, he would produce a work of art that would have a therapeutic effect on himself and his readers. David Gascoyne therefore described surrealist poetry as *a perpetual flow of irrational thought in the form of images*. Much of Dylan Thomas's poetry is similar to this, but it stops short of the surrealist extreme; he made a more deliberate choice of images and looked consciously for images that were either connected or else contradictory.

He explained this process in a much-quoted letter to Henry Treece, an English poet who wrote a stimulating book about Thomas:

> A poem by myself *needs* a host of images, because its centre is a host of images. I make one image — though 'make' is not the word; let, perhaps, an image be 'made' emotionally in me and then apply to it what intellectual and critical forces I possess — let it breed another, let that image contradict the first, make (of the third image bred out of the other two together) a fourth contradictory image, and let them all, within my imposed formal limits, conflict.

Since the process that Thomas describes includes some selection of the images suggested by the subconscious, which are not equally suitable for poetry, he is here insisting that he is a more deliberate craftsman than Gascoyne and other Surrealists. But he gave a more Freudian defence of his art on another occasion when he was asked to write an answer to an enquiry from Geoffrey Grigson: he said that his poetry attempted *the stripping of the individual darkness, which must, inevitably, cast light upon what has been hidden for too long, and by so doing, make clean the naked exposure*; *my poetry*, he continued, *is the record of my individual struggle from darkness towards some measure of light*, and he hoped that it would restore his readers' peace of mind by letting them see more clearly their subconscious impulses.

The range of subjects that he could explore in this way was limited. Many of his images have a sexual significance; for instance, when he writes *The golden shot/Storms in the freezing tomb* he is describing the sperm entering the womb. Indeed he is obsessed by the two ideas that the womb is a kind of tomb, and that the embryo begins to die at the moment when it is conceived. Consequently, sex and death, two of his favourite topics, become inextricably mixed. His third principal topic is religion, and here he appeals strongly to those who wish to believe in a vaguely beneficent power that controls the universe. Others object that if what Thomas has to say is important, it should be unambiguous; they insist that when he concludes a poem with the line — *After the first death, there is no other* he should make it more clear whether he is accepting or denying the Christian doctrine of the Resurrection. The truth is that he frequently mentions God and other words that he heard in chapel as a boy, but never stops to think what he means by them. Often he is so intoxicated by the sound of his lines that the meaning becomes blurred and unimportant.

Besides Thomas's use of vivid, often clashing images, and his obsession with a few favourite themes, his rhetorical poems have other distinctive features. From Gerard Manley Hopkins he copied the use of compound words; most poets would give them hyphens but Thomas often omits them from sheer perversity — his 'Refusal to Mourn' would be greatly improved by a liberal introduction of hyphens. From Hopkins he also copied the use of balanced alliteration, of brilliant play on words, of unusual adjectives that are sometimes puzzling and sometimes thrilling, and of sprung rhythm. This means that the number of accented syllables in a line is fixed, but the number of unaccented syllables varies with the effect that the poet wishes to achieve. In each foot of sprung rhythm there is only one stressed syllable, which must be the first syllable, and may be the only one.

Some of these semi-surrealist poems win us completely with their inspired beginnings, such as:

> *Light breaks where no sun shines:*

But others have more puzzling openings, notably 'January, 1939':

> *Because the pleasure-bird whistles after the hot wires,*
> *Shall the blind horse sing sweeter?*

At first glance this seems a disconcerting example of Thomas's obscurity, but a meaning can be quarried out of it. 'Because the lark sings sweetly after its eyes have been burned out, can we expect the blinded horse to sing?' But the meaning is more complicated: Thomas is condemning the urban wickedness of London which he represents by the symbol of the blinded lark; and the horse blinded by pleasure-seekers is Pegasus, the winged horse of poetry.

Some readers are so thrilled by the compulsive rhetoric of Thomas's more surrealist poetry that they award this the highest praise, as Sir Herbert Read did when he called it *the most absolute poetry that has been written in our time*. Such extreme praise has provoked its critics to opposite extremes of ridicule, such as Amis's bitter gibe that Thomas *should have stuck to spewing beer, not ink*. The truth is that Thomas's semi-surrealist style succeeded on some occasions and failed on others. This general point can be illustrated by taking two detailed examples of one of his characteristic tricks of style — his use of unusual adjectives. When he speaks of *Turning a* petrol *face blind to the enemy*, the epithet is so meaningless as to have little effect, but when in 'A Refusal to Mourn' he leaves the dead child in her grave beside *The unmourning water/Of the* riding *Thames*, the unexpected word not only takes us by surprise but also stresses the flowing movement of the river.

The second (small) group of Thomas's poems are successful in a straightforward way untypical of him. In these he gives a short objective description (usually of a person), develops his thought clearly, and avoids any conflict of images. 'The Hunchback in the Park' gives a vivid picture of the hunchback as he appeared to one of the boys who teased him. 'The Hand that signed the Paper' resembles Auden's 'Embassy' and 'The Managers'; written in 1933, it expressed horror at the power of the modern ruler, and foretold the age of Hiroshima and push-button war. Its epigrammatic polish is untypical of Thomas and it is thus a surprising example of his versatility.

If you appreciate Thomas's original contribution to poetry, but admire it most when it is not too reluctant to achieve a continuous referential meaning, then you will admire most those poems published in *Deaths and Entrances*

(1946) and even later, where he shows that in poetry as well as prose his genius was for contemplating childhood from a distance of time, or where he regrets the actual or imminent death of relations or neighbours. In those poems his images remain striking without becoming obscure. In 'Poem in October' he looks at Laugharne through a sunshine shower, and the present mingles in his memory with mornings long ago. In 'Fern Hill' he writes a poem worthy of comparison with Wordsworth's 'Ode on Intimations of Immortality from Recollections of Early Childhood'; he recreates for us the innocence and happiness of his childhood holidays on his aunt's farm, which seemed like a golden coin minted afresh each dawn. In describing such exhilarating experiences as those in this poem, and in improvising a new style to suit them, Thomas showed real poetic genius.

THE FORCE THAT THROUGH THE GREEN FUSE DRIVES THE FLOWER

THE force that through the green fuse drives the flower
Drives my green age; that blasts the roots of trees
Is my destroyer.
And I am dumb to tell the crooked rose
My youth is bent by the same wintry fever.

The force that drives the water through the rocks
Drives my red blood; that dries the mouthing streams
Turns mine to wax.
And I am dumb to mouth unto my veins
How at the mountain spring the same mouth sucks.   10

The hand that whirls the water in the pool
Stirs the quicksand; that ropes the blowing wind
Hauls my shroud sail.
And I am dumb to tell the hanging man
How of my clay is made the hangman's lime.

The lips of time leech to the fountain head;
Love drips and gathers, but the fallen blood
Shall calm her sores.
And I am dumb to tell a weather's wind
How time has ticked a heaven round the stars.   20

And I am dumb to tell the lover's tomb
How at my sheet goes the same crooked worm.

AND DEATH SHALL HAVE NO DOMINION

AND death shall have no dominion.
Dead men naked they shall be one
With the man in the wind and the west moon;
When their bones are picked clean and the clean bones
    gone,
They shall have stars at elbow and foot;
Though they go mad they shall be sane,
Though they sink through the sea they shall rise again;
Though lovers be lost love shall not;
And death shall have no dominion.

And death shall have no dominion.   10
Under the windings of the sea
They lying long shall not die windily;
Twisting on racks when sinews give way,
Strapped to a wheel, yet they shall not break;
Faith in their hands shall snap in two,
And the unicorn evils run them through;
Split all ends up they shan't crack;
And death shall have no dominion.

And death shall have no dominion.
No more may gulls cry at their ears   20
Or waves break loud on the seashores;
Where blew a flower may a flower no more
Lift its head to the blows of the rain;
Though they be mad and dead as nails,
Heads of the characters hammer through daisies;
Break in the sun till the sun breaks down,
And death shall have no dominion.

THE HAND THAT SIGNED THE PAPER

THE hand that signed the paper felled a city;
Five sovereign fingers taxed the breath,
Doubled the globe of dead and halved a country;
These five kings did a king to death.

The mighty hand leads to a sloping shoulder,
The finger-joints are cramped with chalk;
A goose's quill has put an end to murder
That put an end to talk.

The hand that signed the treaty bred a fever,
And famine grew, and locusts came;   10
Great is the hand that holds dominion over
Man by a scribbled name.

The five kings count the dead but do not soften
The crusted wound nor stroke the brow;
A hand rules pity as a hand rules heaven;
Hands have no tears to flow.

POEM IN OCTOBER

IT was my thirtieth year to heaven
Woke to my hearing from harbour and neighbour wood
    And the mussel pooled and the heron
            Priested shore
        The morning beckon
With water praying and call of seagull and rook
And the knock of sailing boats on the net webbed wall
        Myself to set foot
            That second
    In the still sleeping town and set forth.   10

My birthday began with the water-
Birds and the birds of the winged trees flying my name
   Above the farms and the white horses
      And I rose
     In rainy autumn
And walked abroad in a shower of all my days.
High tide and the heron dived when I took the road
   Over the border
     And the gates
Of the town closed as the town awoke.   20

A springful of larks in a rolling
Cloud and the roadside bushes brimming with whistling
   Blackbirds and the sun of October
      Summery
     On the hill's shoulder,
Here were fond climates and sweet singers suddenly
Come in the morning where I wandered and listened
   To the rain wringing
     Wind blow cold
In the wood faraway under me.   30

Pale rain over the dwindling harbour
And over the sea wet church the size of a snail
   With its horns through mist and the castle
      Brown as owls
     But all the gardens
Of spring and summer were blooming in the tall tales
Beyond the border and under the lark full cloud.
   There could I marvel
     My birthday
Away but the weather turned around.   40

It turned away from the blithe country
And down the other air and the blue altered sky
   Streamed again a wonder of summer
      With apples
     Pears and red currants

And I saw in the turning so clearly a child's
Forgotten mornings when he walked with his mother
    Through the parables
        Of sunlight
    And the legends of the green chapels   50

And the twice told fields of infancy
That his tears burned my cheeks and his heart moved in
    mine.
    These were the woods the river and sea
        Where a boy
    In the listening
Summertime of the dead whispered the truth of his joy
To the trees and the stones and the fish in the tide.
    And the mystery
        Sang alive
Still in the water and singingbirds.   60

And there could I marvel my birthday
Away but the weather turned around. And the true
    Joy of the long dead child sang burning
        In the sun.
    It was my thirtieth
Year to heaven stood there then in the summer noon
Though the town below lay leaved with October blood.
    O may my heart's truth
        Still be sung
On this high hill in a year's turning.   70

FERN HILL

Now as I was young and easy under the apple boughs
About the lilting house and happy as the grass was green,
    The night above the dingle starry,
        Time let me hail and climb
    Golden in the heydays of his eyes,

And honoured among wagons I was prince of the apple
    towns
And once below a time I lordly had the trees and leaves
    Trail with daisies and barley
  Down the rivers of the windfall light.

And as I was green and carefree, famous among the
    barns   10
About the happy yard and singing as the farm was home,
  In the sun that is young once only,
    Time let me play and be
  Golden in the mercy of his means,
And green and golden I was huntsman and herdsman,
    the calves
Sang to my horn, the foxes on the hills barked clear and
    cold,
    And the sabbath rang slowly
  In the pebbles of the holy streams.

All the sun long it was running, it was lovely, the hay
Fields high as the house, the tunes from the chimneys, it
    was air   20
  And playing, lovely and watery
    And fire green as grass.
  And nightly under the simple stars
As I rode to sleep the owls were bearing the farm away,
All the moon long I heard, blessed among stables, the
    night-jars
    Flying with the ricks, and the horses
  Flashing into the dark.

And then to awake, and the farm, like a wanderer white
With the dew, come back, the cock on his shoulder: it
    was all
  Shining, it was Adam and maiden,   30
    The sky gathered again
  And the sun grew round that very day.
So it must have been after the birth of the simple light

In the first, spinning place, the spellbound horses walking
　　warm
　　　Out of the whinnying green stable
　　On to the fields of praise.

And honoured among foxes and pheasants by the gay
　　house
Under the new made clouds and happy as the heart was
　　long,
　　　In the sun born over and over,
　　　　I ran my heedless ways,   40
　　My wishes raced through the house high hay
And nothing I cared, at my sky blue trades, that time
　　allows
In all his tuneful turning so few and such morning songs
　　　Before the children green and golden
　　Follow him out of grace,

Nothing I cared, in the lamb white days, that time would
　　take me
Up to the swallow thronged loft by the shadow of my
　　hand,
　　　In the moon that is always rising,
　　　　Nor that riding to sleep
　　I should hear him fly with the high fields   50
And wake to the farm forever fled from the childless land.
Oh as I was young and easy in the mercy of his means,
　　　Time held me green and dying
　　Though I sang in my chains like the sea.

THE HUNCHBACK IN THE PARK

　　　The hunchback in the park
　　　A solitary mister
　　　Propped between trees and water
　　　From the opening of the garden lock

That lets the trees and water enter
Until the Sunday sombre bell at dark

Eating bread from a newspaper
Drinking water from the chained cup
That the children filled with gravel
In the fountain basin where I sailed my ship   10
Slept at night in a dog kennel
But nobody chained him up.

Like the park birds he came early
Like the water he sat down
And Mister they called Hey mister
The truant boys from the town
Running when he had heard them clearly
On out of sound

Past lake and rockery
Laughing when he shook his paper   20
Hunchbacked in mockery
Through the loud zoo of the willow groves
Dodging the park keeper
With his stick that picked up leaves.

And the old dog sleeper
Alone between nurses and swans
While the boys among willows
Made the tigers jump out of their eyes
To roar on the rockery stones
And the groves were blue with sailors   30

Made all day until bell time
A woman figure without fault
Straight as a young elm
Straight and tall from his crooked bones
That she might stand in the night
After the locks and chains

All night in the unmade park
After the railings and shrubberies
The birds the grass the trees the lake
And the wild boys innocent as strawberries   40
Had followed the hunchback
To his kennel in the dark.

IN MY CRAFT OR SULLEN ART

In my craft or sullen art
Exercised in the still night
When only the moon rages
And the lovers lie abed
With all their griefs in their arms,
I labour by singing light
Not for ambition or bread
Or the strut and trade of charms
On the ivory stages
But for the common wages   10
Of their most secret heart.

Not for the proud man apart
From the raging moon I write
On these spindrift pages
Nor for the towering dead
With their nightingales and psalms
But for the lovers, their arms
Round the griefs of the ages,
Who pay no praise or wages
Nor heed my craft or art.   20

A REFUSAL TO MOURN THE DEATH, BY FIRE,
OF A CHILD IN LONDON

NEVER until the mankind making
Bird beast and flower
Fathering and all humbling darkness
Tells with silence the last light breaking
And the still hour
Is come of the sea tumbling in harness

And I must enter again the round
Zion of the water bead
And the synagogue of the ear of corn
Shall I let pray the shadow of a sound   10
Or sow my salt seed
In the least valley of sackcloth to mourn

The majesty and burning of the child's death.
I shall not murder
The mankind of her going with a grave truth
Nor blaspheme down the stations of the breath
With any further
Elegy of innocence and youth.

Deep with the first dead lies London's daughter,
Robed in the long friends,   20
The grains beyond age, the dark veins of her mother,
Secret by the unmourning water
Of the riding Thames.
After the first death, there is no other.

DO NOT GO GENTLE INTO
THAT GOOD NIGHT

Do not go gentle into that good night,
Old age should burn and rave at close of day;
Rage, rage against the dying of the light.

Though wise men at their end know dark is right,
Because their words had forked no lightning they
Do not go gentle into that good night.

Good men, the last wave by, crying how bright
Their frail deeds might have danced in a green bay,
Rage, rage against the dying of the light.

Wild men who caught and sang the sun in flight,   10
And learn, too late, they grieved it on its way,
Do not go gentle into that good night.

Grave men, near death, who see with blinding sight
Blind eyes could blaze like meteors and be gay,
Rage, rage against the dying of the light.

And you, my father, there on the sad height,
Curse, bless, me now with your fierce tears, I pray.
Do not go gentle into that good night.
Rage, rage against the dying of the light.

PHILIP LARKIN

WITHOUT accepting the cynical view that fashions in poetry swing from one extreme to another, one can regard it as inevitable that a new generation would try to present the contemporary scene with less obscurity than Eliot — or even Auden — had done. The young poets of the 1950's set out to write poetry that had a more obvious sense of form, rhythms that were easier to recognise, and a meaning that was more precise and definite. They were so afraid of appearing to imitate Auden that they resolved to be deliberately different from him, for though they admired his technical virtuosity, they resented his determination to use poetry as a manifesto of his ethical ideas, whether Marxist or Christian. They accepted the negative opinions of T. S. Eliot, the critic, about the kinds of poetry that ought not to be written in this century, but they did not find T. S. Eliot, the poet, of much help as a model.

In October 1954 an article in *The Spectator* announced a new trend in poetry, which it called 'The Movement'. The writers who belonged to it represented an intellectual reaction against the neo-romantics of the 1940's, especially Dylan Thomas, whose death they thought had been mourned too extravagantly. They demanded that intelligence and intelligibility should be regarded as essential virtues in poetry.

The effect of this *Spectator* article was reinforced in 1956 when Robert Conquest published an anthology, *New Lines*, which seemed to give unity and consistency to the Movement, and created for its members a recognisable public image. In his introduction Conquest recalled that the typical poets of the 1930's (Auden and his friends) and those of the 1940's (Dylan Thomas and his imitators) had been launched by anthologies that took up definite positions. He was consciously trying to do the same for 1956 and the years ahead; he was presenting to the public a group of nine poets who wrote *a genuine and healthy poetry* that belonged unmistakably to a new period. They were Elizabeth Jennings, John Holloway, Philip Larkin, Thomas Gunn, Kingsley Amis, D. J. Enright, Donald Davie, John Wain and himself. Six of them were (at that time) university lecturers, two were librarians and one was a civil servant. Their poetry was intelligent, knowledgeable and polished. They were resolved to avoid the faults of Dylan Thomas, whom Conquest accused of destroying the taste of the poetry-reading public and insisting on the debilitating theory that poetry *must* be metaphorical. In contrast to Thomas, Conquest declared, these poets would not surrender their technical excellence in order to explore the sub-conscious, and he condemned Thomas for being content to make *an arrangement of images of sex or violence tapped straight from the unconscious (a sort of upper-middle-brow horror comic), or to evoke without comment the naivetés and nostalgias of childhood*. (This last phrase is a preposterous and unnecessary denigration of poems such as 'Fern Hill'.)

Conquest went on to make a more positive statement of the qualities that the new poets shared:

> In one sense, indeed, the standpoint is not new, but merely the restoration of a sound and fruitful attitude to poetry, of the principle that poetry is written by and for the whole man, intellect, emotions, senses and all. But restorations are not repetitions. The atmosphere, the attack of these poets is as concentratedly contemporary as could be imagined. To be of one's own time is not an important virtue, but it is a necessary one.
>
> If one had briefly to distinguish this poetry of the fifties from its predecessors, I believe the most important general point would be that it submits to no great systems of theoretical constructs nor agglomerations of unconscious commands. It is free from both mystical and logical compulsions and — like modern philosophy

— is empirical in its attitude to all that comes. . . . On the more technical side, though of course related to all this, we see refusal to abandon a rational structure and comprehensible language, even when the verse is most highly charged with sensuous or emotional intent.

Of the writers whom Conquest championed, Philip Larkin has achieved most as a poet, whilst Amis and Wain have been more successful as novelists. Larkin was born in 1922 in Coventry, where his father was Town Clerk (though in 'I Remember, I Remember' he refuses to be sentimental about his native town). As a student at St. John's College, Oxford he became a close friend of Kingsley Amis, who later dedicated *Lucky Jim* (1954) to him, and whose daughter Sally was to be the subject of Larkin's poem, 'Born Yesterday'. Since 1943 he has held various posts in university libraries and in 1955 he became Librarian of the University of Hull. Like Amis, Larkin is very interested in jazz, and he has been jazz correspondent of the *Daily Telegraph*. His two novels, *Jill* (1946) and *A Girl in Winter* (1947) are beginning to convince critics that they deserve more attention than they received at first. In poems such as 'The Whitsun Weddings' Larkin makes skilful use of his novelist's knack of choosing touches of detail that give just the right effect, such as the girls gripping their handbags tighter as they throw confetti at the honeymoon couples boarding the train, and the brides' fathers wearing broad belts under their suits as they see them off.

The virtues of Larkin's poetry are clarity and elegance. He has a reliable instinct for orderly arrangement, and a respect for formal perfection. He makes the most of his gifts, and has an accurate sense of his limitations. His skilful craftsmanship enables him to build up a firm structure in his poems and to portray the realistic details of the contemporary scene in language that has a recognisable rhythm and a consistent polish. In poetry that fits naturally into rhymed and obviously metrical verse, and

which inherits the traditional virtues of poetry as a medium
of artistic expression, he takes a thoughtful look at England
as it really is. 'The Whitsun Weddings' begins with a
convincing glimpse of Hull as he leaves it on a train:

> *We ran*
>
> *Behind the backs of houses, crossed a street*
> *Of blinding windscreens, smelt the fish-dock; thence*
> *The river's level drifting breadth began,*
> *Where sky and Lincolnshire and water meet.*

As the train speeds south, he catches a series of realistic
views of the towns that the train rushes through, seeing
Canals with floatings of industrial froth and then *Acres of
dismantled cars.* Such lines are more than accurate photography; they suggest how shallow and spiritually im-
poverished are the lives of many of the people who live in
these surroundings. A different example of Larkin's gift of
terse, concrete phrases is *Snow fell, undated,* which indicates
briefly and vividly how swift and vague the passage of time
became to husband and wife in their tomb. The definite
details presented by such lines are combined in poems that
develop ideas logically as well as having a regular stanza
structure. 'The Whitsun Weddings' progresses from his
impressions of Hull, and the towns he passes through, to
his growing awareness of the bridal couples joining the
train. He develops a contrast between the pre-occupied
young couples, who merely *watched* the landscape, and the
bachelor poet who sits back in the corner of his compart-
ment, sees and understands the actions of the different
couples, and harmonises their various experiences into a
unified impression, just as a composer unites a number of
themes into a complete orchestral harmony. He turns their
experiences into something more complete.

Similarly 'Church Going' begins with a picture of the
unassuming poet on a bicycle hesitating to enter a church
and feeling a little afraid of experts on architecture who
know so much more than he does about church roofs. The
poem proceeds systematically to express Larkin's notion of

a future in which churches will be abandoned, and then comes to an emotional ending that regrets so serious a break with our cultural traditions.

The sense of form that these poems illustrate is one of the positive qualities that makes Larkin's poetry noticeably different from that of the Romantics whether they are Wordsworth and Coleridge or Dylan Thomas and Henry Treece. His rejection of romanticism also has its negative features, such as his flat contradiction, in 'I Remember, I Remember', of the idea that *Heaven lies about us in our infancy*. Some of his poetry reflects the anti-heroic mood of the 1950's when the 'cold war' seemed to have frozen most illusions to death, when even university lecturers wrote novels as flippant as *Lucky Jim*, and when poets felt that in order to make a statement of positive values they had first to clear away the debris of cant and convention. Consequently it is tempting to express appreciation of Larkin's poetry by slipping into negatives; it is tempting to praise him for not ignoring or distorting syntax in the way that Eliot did, for not trying to convert us to an inconsistent series of causes as Auden did, and for not dredging up the debris of images from his subconscious as Dylan Thomas did. But such criticism is not only unfair to these earlier poets, whose achievement cannot be shrivelled up by a few epigrams; but it is also unfair to Larkin too, because there is nothing negative or inhibited about his poetry. It makes interesting a variety of topics about which the poets of Auden's generation had surprisingly little to say, but which we recognise as important parts of the world around us. Larkin writes about them in language that is not only lucid and memorable, but is natural and forceful too. And he gives the impression of being a friendly, sensible person whose comments on life and people are both sympathetic and stimulating.

It is therefore understandable that Larkin has won considerable acclaim. For instance, in 1973 he was invited to edit *The Oxford Book of Twentieth-Century Verse*; in 1965 he was awarded the Queen's Gold Medal for Poetry; and in 1975 he was awarded the CBE.

MAIDEN NAME

MARRYING left your maiden name disused.
Its five light sounds no longer mean your face,
Your voice, and all your variants of grace;
For since you were so thankfully confused
By law with someone else, you cannot be
Semantically the same as that young beauty:
It was of her that these two words were used.

Now it's a phrase, applicable to no one,
Lying just where you left it, scattered through
Old lists, old programmes, a school prize or two,   10
Packets of letters tied with tartan ribbon —
Then is it scentless, weightless, strengthless, wholly
Untruthful? Try whispering it slowly.
No, it means you. Or, since you're past and gone,

It means what we feel now about you then:
How beautiful you were, and near, and young,
So vivid, you might still be there among
Those first few days, unfingermarked again.
So your old name shelters our faithfulness,
Instead of losing shape and meaning less   20
With your depreciating luggage laden.

I REMEMBER, I REMEMBER

COMING up England by a different line
For once, early in the cold new year,
We stopped and watching men with number-plates
Sprint down the platform to familiar gates,
'Why, Coventry!' I exclaimed. 'I was born here'.

I leant far out and squinnied for a sign
That this was still the town that had been 'Mine'
So long, but found I wasn't even clear
Which side was which. From where those cycle-crates
Were standing, had we annually departed   10

For all those family hols? . . . A whistle went:
Things moved. I sat back, staring at my boots.
'Was that', my friend smiled, 'where you "have your
        roots"?'
No, only where my childhood was unspent,
I wanted to retort, just where I started:

By now I've got the whole place clearly charted.
Our garden, first: where I did not invent
Blinding theologies of flowers and fruits,
And wasn't spoken to by an old hat.
And here we have that splendid family   20

I never ran to when I got depressed,
The boys all biceps and the girls all chest,
Their comic Ford, their farm, where I could be
'Really myself'. I'll show you, come to that,
The bracken where I never trembling sat,

Determined to go through with it; where she
Lay back, and 'all became a burning mist'.
And, in those offices, my doggerel
Was not set up in blunt ten-point, nor read
By a distinguished cousin of the mayor,   30

Who didn't call and tell my father *There
Before us, had we the gift to see ahead* —
'You look as if you wished the place in Hell,'
My friend said, 'judging from your face.' 'Oh well,
I suppose it's not the place's fault,' I said.

'Nothing, like something, happens anywhere.'

CHURCH GOING

ONCE I am sure there's nothing going on
I step inside, letting the door thud shut.
Another church: matting, seats, and stone,
And little books; sprawlings of flowers, cut
For Sunday, brownish now; some brass and stuff
Up at the holy end; the small neat organ;
And a tense, musty, unignorable silence,
Brewed God knows how long. Hatless, I take off
My cycle-clips in awkward reverence,

Move forward, run my hand around the font.   10
From where I stand, the roof looks almost new —
Cleaned, or restored? Someone would know: I don't.
Mounting the lectern, I peruse a few
Hectoring large-scale verses, and pronounce
'Here endeth' much more loudly than I'd meant.
The echoes snigger briefly. Back at the door
I sign the book, donate an Irish sixpence,
Reflect the place was not worth stopping for.

Yet stop I did: in fact I often do,
And always end much at a loss like this,   20
Wondering what to look for; wondering, too,
When churches fall completely out of use
What we shall turn them into, if we shall keep
A few cathedrals chronically on show,
Their parchment, plate and pyx in locked cases,
And let the rest rent-free to rain and sheep.
Shall we avoid them as unlucky places?

Or, after dark, will dubious women come
To make their children touch a particular stone;
Pick simples for a cancer; or on some   30
Advised night see walking a dead one?

Power of some sort or other will go on
In games, in riddles, seemingly at random;
But superstition, like belief, must die,
And what remains when disbelief has gone?
Grass, weedy pavement, brambles, buttress, sky,

A shape less recognizable each week,
A purpose more obscure. I wonder who
Will be the last, the very last, to seek
This place for what it was; one of the crew   40
That tap and jot and know what rood-lofts were?
Some ruin-bibber, randy for antique,
Or Christmas-addict, counting on a whiff
Of gown-and-bands and organ-pipes and myrrh?
Or will he be my representative,

Bored, uninformed, knowing the ghostly silt
Dispersed, yet tending to this cross of ground
Through suburb scrub because it held unspilt
So long and equably what since is found
Only in separation — marriage, and birth,   50
And death, and thoughts of these — for which was built
This special shell? For, though I've no idea
What this accoutred frowsty barn is worth,
It pleases me to stand in silence here;

A serious house on serious earth it is,
In whose blent air all our compulsions meet,
Are recognised, and robed as destinies.
And that much never can be obsolete,
Since someone will forever be surprising
A hunger in himself to be more serious,   60
And gravitating with it to this ground,
Which, he once heard, was proper to grow wise in,
If only that so many dead lie round.

THE WHITSUN WEDDINGS

THAT Whitsun, I was late getting away:
   Not till about
One-twenty on the sunlit Saturday
Did my three-quarters-empty train pull out,
All windows down, all cushions hot, all sense
Of being in a hurry gone. We ran
Behind the backs of houses, crossed a street
Of blinding windscreens, smelt the fish-dock; thence
The river's level drifting breadth began,
Where sky and Lincolnshire and water meet.   10

All afternoon, through the tall heat that slept
   For miles inland,
A slow and stopping curve southwards we kept.
Wide farms went by, short-shadowed cattle, and
Canals with floatings of industrial froth;
A hothouse flashed, uniquely; hedges dipped
And rose; and now and then a smell of grass
Displaced the reek of buttoned carriage-cloth
Until the next town, new and nondescript,
Approached with acres of dismantled cars.   20

At first, I didn't notice what a noise
   The weddings made
Each station that we stopped at: sun destroys
The interest of what's happening in the shade,
And down the long cool platforms whoops and skirls
I took for porters larking with the mails
And went on reading. Once we started, though,
We passed them grinning and pomaded, girls
In parodies of fashion, heels and veils,
All posed irresolutely, watching us go,   30

As if out on the end of an event
   Waving good-bye
To something that survived it. Struck, I leant
More promptly out next time, more curiously,
And saw it all again in different terms:
The fathers with broad belts under their suits
And seamy foreheads; mothers loud and fat;
An uncle shouting smut; and then the perms,
The nylon gloves and jewellery-substitutes,
The lemons, mauves, and olive-ochres that   40

Marked off the girls unreally from the rest.
   Yes, from cafés
And banquet-halls up yards, and bunting-dressed
Coach-party annexes, the wedding-days
Were coming to an end. All down the line
Fresh couples climbed aboard; the rest stood round;
The last confetti and advice were thrown,
And, as we moved, each face seemed to define
Just what it saw departing: children frowned
At something dull; fathers had never known   50

Success so huge and wholly farcical;
   The women shared
The secret like a happy funeral;
While girls, gripping their handbags tighter, stared
At a religious wounding. Free at last,
And loaded with the sum of all they saw,
We hurried towards London, shuffling gouts of steam.
Now fields were building-plots, and poplars cast
Long shadows over major roads, and for
Some fifty minutes, that in time would seem   60

Just long enough to settle hats and say
   I nearly died
A dozen marriages got under way.
They watched the landscape, sitting side by side
— An Odeon went past, a cooling tower,

And someone running up to bowl — and none
Thought of the others they would never meet
Or how their lives would all contain this hour.
I thought of London spread out in the sun,
Its postal districts packed like squares of wheat: 70

There we were aimed. And as we raced across
    Bright knots of rail
Past standing Pullmans, walls of blackened moss
Came close, and it was nearly done, this frail
Travelling coincidence; and what it held
Stood ready to be loosed with all the power
That being changed can give. We slowed again,
And as the tightened brakes took hold, there swelled
A sense of falling, like an arrow-shower
Sent out of sight, somewhere becoming rain.   80

AT GRASS

THE eye can hardly pick them out
From the cold shade they shelter in,
Till wind distresses tail and mane;
Then one crops grass, and moves about
— The other seeming to look on —
And stands anonymous again.

Yet fifteen years ago, perhaps
Two dozen distances sufficed
To fable them: faint afternoons
Of Cups and Stakes and Handicaps,   10
Whereby their names were artificed
To inlay faded, classic Junes —

Silks at the start: against the sky
Numbers and parasols: outside,

Squadrons of empty cars, and heat,
And littered grass : then the long cry
Hanging unhushed till it subside
To stop-press columns on the street.

Do memories plague their ears like flies ?
They shake their heads. Dusk brims the shadows.   20
Summer by summer all stole away,
The starting-gates, the crowds and cries —
All but the unmolesting meadows.
Almanacked, their names live; they

Have slipped their names, and stand at ease,
Or gallop for what must be joy,
And not a fieldglass sees them home,
Or curious stop-watch prophesies :
Only the groom, and the groom's boy,
With bridles in the evening come.   30

LINES ON A YOUNG LADY'S
PHOTOGRAPH ALBUM

At last you yielded up the album, which
Once open, sent me distracted. All your ages
Matt and glossy on the thick black pages !
Too much confectionery, too rich :
I choke on such nutritious images.

My swivel eye hungers from pose to pose —
In pigtails, clutching a reluctant cat;
Or furred yourself, a sweet girl-graduate;
Or lifting a heavy-headed rose
Beneath a trellis, or in a trilby hat   10

(Faintly disturbing, that, in several ways) —
From every side you strike at my control,

Not least through these disquieting chaps who loll
At ease about your earlier days:
Not quite your class, I'd say, dear, on the whole.

But o, photography! as no art is,
Faithful and disappointing! that records
Dull days as dull, and hold-it smiles as frauds,
And will not censor blemishes
Like washing-lines, and Hall's Distemper boards,   20

But shows the cat as disinclined, and shades
A chin as doubled when it is, what grace
Your candour thus confers upon her face!
How overwhelmingly persuades
That this is a real girl in a real place,

In every sense empirically true!
Or is it just *the past*? Those flowers, that gate,
These misty parks and motors, lacerate
Simply by being over; you
Contract my heart by looking out of date.   30

Yes, true; but in the end, surely, we cry
Not only at exclusion, but because
It leaves us free to cry. We know *what was*
Won't call on us to justify
Our grief, however hard we yowl across

The gap from eye to page. So I am left
To mourn (without a chance of consequence)
You, balanced on a bike against a fence;
To wonder if you'd spot the theft
Of this one of you bathing; to condense,   40

In short, a past that no one now can share,
No matter whose your future; calm and dry,
It holds you like a heaven, and you lie
Unvariably lovely there,
Smaller and clearer as the years go by.

WEDDING WIND

THE wind blew all my wedding-day,
And my wedding-night was the night of the high wind;
And a stable door was banging, again and again,
That he must go and shut it, leaving me
Stupid in candlelight, hearing rain,
Seeing my face in the twisted candlestick,
Yet seeing nothing. When he came back
He said the horses were restless, and I was sad
That any man or beast that night should lack
The happiness I had.
                              Now in the day   10
All's ravelled under the sun by the wind's blowing.
He has gone to look at the floods, and I
Carry a chipped pail to the chicken-run,
Set it down, and stare. All is the wind
Hunting through clouds and forests, thrashing
My apron and the hanging cloths on the line.
Can it be borne, this bodying-forth by wind
Of joy my actions turn on, like a thread
Carrying beads? Shall I be let to sleep
Now this perpetual morning shares my bed?   20
Can even death dry up
These new delighted lakes, conclude
Our kneeling as cattle by all-generous waters?

NEXT, PLEASE

ALWAYS too eager for the future, we
Pick up bad habits of expectancy.
Something is always approaching; every day
Till then we say,

Watching from a bluff the tiny, clear,
Sparkling armada of promises draw near.
How slow they are! And how much time they waste,
Refusing to make haste!

Yet still they leave us holding wretched stalks
Of disappointment, for, though nothing balks   10
Each big approach, leaning with brasswork prinked,
Each rope distinct,

Flagged and the figurehead with golden tits
Arching our way, it never anchors; it's
No sooner than it turns to past.
Right to the last

We think each one will heave to and unload
All good into our lives, all we are owed
For waiting so devoutly and so long.
But we are wrong: 20

Only one ship is seeking us, a black-
Sailed unfamiliar, towing at her back
A huge and birdless silence. In her wake
No waters breed or break.

TOADS

Why should I let the toad *work*
    Squat on my life?
Can't I use my wit as a pitchfork
    And drive the brute off?

Six days of the week it soils
    With its sickening poison —
Just for paying a few bills!
    That's out of proportion.

Lots of folk live on their wits:
    Lecturers, lispers,   10
Losels, loblolly-men, louts —
    They don't end as paupers;

Lots of folk live up lanes
    With fires in a bucket,
Eat windfalls and tinned sardines —
    They seem to like it.

Their nippers have got bare feet,
    Their unspeakable wives
Are skinny as whippets — and yet
    No one actually *starves*.   20

Ah, were I courageous enough
    To shout *Stuff your pension*!
But I know, all too well, that's the stuff
    That dreams are made on:

For something sufficiently toad-like
    Squats in me, too;
Its hunkers are heavy as hard luck,
    And cold as snow,

And will never allow me to blarney
    My way to getting   30
The fame and the girl and the money
    All at one sitting.

I don't say, one bodies the other
    One's spiritual truth;
But I do say it's hard to lose either,
    When you have both.

AN ARUNDEL TOMB

SIDE by side, their faces blurred,
The earl and countess lie in stone,
Their proper habits vaguely shown
As jointed armour, stiffened pleat,
And that faint hint of the absurd —
The little dogs under their feet.

Such plainness of the pre-baroque
Hardly involves the eye, until
It meets his left-hand gauntlet, still
Clasped empty in the other; and
One sees, with a sharp tender shock,
His hand withdrawn, holding her hand.

They would not think to lie so long.
Such faithfulness in effigy
Was just a detail friends would see:
A sculptor's sweet commissioned grace
Thrown off in helping to prolong
The Latin names around the base.

They would not guess how early in
Their supine stationary voyage
The air would change to soundless damage,
Turn the old tenantry away;
How soon succeeding eyes begin
To look, not read. Rigidly they

Persisted, linked, through lengths and breadths
Of time. Snow fell, undated. Light
Each summer thronged the glass. A bright
Litter of birdcalls strewed the same
Bone-riddled ground. And up the paths
The endless altered people came,

10

20

30

Washing at their identity.
Now, helpless in the hollow of
An unarmorial age, a trough
Of smoke in slow suspended skeins
Above their scrap of history,
Only an attitude remains:

Time has transfigured them into
Untruth. The stone fidelity
They hardly meant has come to be
Their final blazon, and to prove   40
Our almost-instinct almost true:
What will survive of us is love.

TED HUGHES

TED HUGHES was born in 1930, and may write some of his best poems in the future. He was born in Mytholmroyd, a small town on the Yorkshire slopes of the Pennines.

He was educated at Mexborough Grammar School and Pembroke College, Cambridge. He tried an unconventional variety of jobs, working, for instance, as a gardener and a night-watchman. In 1956 he married the poetess Sylvia Plath; in 1957 he visited America where he was able to make a living by writing and teaching. On his return to England in 1957 Hughes found that his first volume of poems, *The Hawk in the Rain*, was Poetry Book Society Choice and had been much praised by the critics.

His second volume of poems, *Lupercal* (published in 1960), takes its name from the festival of the Roman wolf-god. The Romans believed that if the priests and their helpers struck a barren woman with their whips, it would bestow fertility on her. Shakespeare's Julius Caesar says to Mark Antony on the day of this feast:

> Forget not, in your speed, Antonius,
> To touch Calpurnia; for our elders say,
> The barren, touched in this holy chase,
> Shake off their sterile curse.

Presumably Hughes believes that his poetry, like the whips of the priests, may help in remedying the barrenness of modern civilisation. His poem 'February', which is semi-autobiographical, expresses the attitudes of a man who is obsessed by a photograph of the *hairless, knuckled feet of the last wolf killed in Britain*; these feet represent some positive power that the modern world has lost. Hughes's picture of this man who is so obsessed with images and visions of wolves that *he sits making wolf-masks* is an indirect portrait of the poet himself, who tries by writing poems about wolves and other animals to revitalise the world.

Hughes obviously has some affinities with D. H. Lawrence. His poems about animals show the sort of sympathy with them that D. H. Lawrence shows in his poems *Bat* and *Snake*; more important, they share Lawrence's admiration of the essential sanity and goodness of our instinctive impulses. In Lawrence's autobiographical novel, *Sons and Lovers*, we see the tragic conflict between the virtues of the mother and the very different virtues of the father (both characters being portraits of Lawrence's own parents). He describes the instinctive warmth of his father, an uneducated miner, and how his father's generous vitality attracted his mother to begin with: *Therefore the dusky, golden softness of this man's sensuous flame of life, that flowed off his flesh like flame from a candle, not baffled and gripped into incandescence by thought and spirit as her life was, seemed to her something wonderful, beyond her.*

Hughes admires similar positive qualities in the animals that he describes. As the critic Alvarez shows, the horses in Hughes's poem 'A Dream of Horses' remind us of the strange, savage horses which terrorise Ursula Brangwen at the end of *The Rainbow*.

Ted Hughes, having been born in the same sort of semi-industrialised area as Lawrence (where pits or mills are next to cornfields, and natural beauty struggles to survive alongside the drabbest slag-heaps), has a Lawrentian sympathy for the more violent and elemental human impulses. He writes so often about animals and birds because he finds in them the unsophisticated vitality that urban man is in danger of losing. The hawk or the otter, trying (often in vain) to survive the murderous attacks of man, symbolises the attempt of beauty, passion, and natural vital instincts to survive in an artificial society. *What excites my imagination*, he once said, *is the war between vitality and death.*

He excels in ingenious ways of finding words for physical shocks and sensations such as *the sudden sharp hot stink of fox*, or in words that brilliantly suggest action as when the otter 'Re-enters the water by *melting*' or the macaw *bristles in a staring/Combustion.*

In 'A Dream of Horses' both the narrator and Hughes himself are fascinated, obsessed and terrified by the horses and their violence. The sharp, convincing details of the description give them a compelling presence. These horses dominate the lives and thoughts of the grooms till they think of the fires of the Day of Judgement as taking the shapes of horses and they think of the future life (*the forever*) as being full of horses' hooves. The horses that the grooms dream of are frighteningly real as is the fear they create.

Others of Hughes's best poems are dominated by an element of shock and violence; they find remarkable verbal expression for powerful physical sensations, and are inspired by a fervent admiration of the wild creatures that they describe. But his great success is in communicating to his readers his admiration of animals' energetic life-force.

As A. E. Dyson wrote in *The Critical Quarterly*, 'The major theme in the poems is power; and power thought of not morally, or in time, but absolutely — in a present which is often violent and self-destructive, but isolated from motive or consequence, and so unmodified by the irony which time confers. For Ted Hughes power and violence go together: his own dark gods are makers of the tiger, not the lamb. He is fascinated by violence of all kinds, in love and in hatred, in the jungle and the arena, in battle, murder and sudden death. Violence, for him, is the occasion not for reflection, but for being; it is a guarantee of energy, of life.'

In 'The Jaguar' Hughes admires the jaguar who is so active and defiant, who does not give up the struggle as the yawning apes and the indolent lion do, and who mesmerises the crowd at the zoo with his fiery eyes and wild stride. In 'Macaw and Little Miss' he is impressed by the granddaughter when she dreams of a lover who will show the warrior qualities that the macaw does; for when the girl strikes the cage in a tantrum the macaw retaliates:

Instantly beak, wings, talons crash
The bars in conflagration and frenzy,
And his shriek shakes the house.

In 'Esther's Tomcat' Hughes begins with the image of
the cat asleep in the daytime *stretched flat as an old rough cat*,
but ends by admiring the same cat at night when it
becomes an ageless green-eyed 'unkillable' cat (that once
killed a knight). *An Otter* achieves a similar contrast in
reverse: Hughes begins with a list of the various abilities of
the otter, but ends with the sad picture of it when it *reverts
to nothing at all,/To this long pelt over the back of a chair.* Hughes
implies that it is a loss to the world.

The poems that present these animals and birds are
among his very best because they concentrate on a single
animal or bird and cohere round a single theme. The
imagery is forceful and striking, and intellectually disciplined to drive home a limited number of relevant ideas.

The most obvious feature of Hughes's style is his use of
violent, unusual phrases. His poetry has the youthful
vigour that we associate with Marlowe, and the love of
verbal acrobatics, such as using nouns as verbs, that we
associate with Gerard Manley Hopkins or Dylan Thomas.
For instance, Grooms *drank* the din, darkness was *avalanching*,
apes *adore* their fleas, and the wind *dented* the balls of
Hughes's eyes. An ingenious line (*By the bang of blood in the
brain deaf the ear*) makes us hear the blood throbbing in the
head of the furious jaguar till it cannot hear the crowd;
the monosyllables make the blood-beat audible.

Though Hughes is so fond of wild animals, he has
learnt from Donne and Eliot how to describe them in a
witty, sophisticated way. He makes his readers sit up and
notice his unusual similes, such as when he describes *a black
Back gull bent like an iron bar*, or an aged macaw hanging
Like a torturer's iron instrument. With a kind of 'metaphysical'
wit he describes the tiger and lion in the zoo *as fatigued with
indolence*. Consequently, he shares R. S. Thomas's gift of
being able to write about the country and country life as

though he had never read any nineteenth-century poetry about it. His style is as modern as his ideas about animals are realistic and unsentimental. He continues to write honestly about the brutality of the natural world. But he believes that modern agriculture does not need to be so destructive and he is enthusiastic about farming techniques that will conserve the countryside.

For all these reasons his poetry has been widely accepted and warmly praised for its vitality. In recognition, he was awarded the OBE in 1977 and in 1984 he was appointed Poet Laureate.

Tragically, Sylvia Plath committed suicide in 1963. In 1970 he married Carol Orchard and went to live in Devon. As well as writing poetry for adults, he has written a great deal of poetry for children and he has attached considerable importance to giving poetry readings in schools and doing all that he can to encourage the active enjoyment of poetry in schools.

In 1971 Hughes published *Crow*. His harsher critics accused him of inventing imaginary animals, or of writing again about old favourites such as the Jaguar — they condemned him for not writing very often or very well about humans. They accused him of bludgeoning his readers with rhetorical references to blood and death.

A problem that is difficult to answer is this — when Hughes writes about a wild animal (or bird) is he really writing about that animal (or bird) or is he using the bird as a symbol for some human characteristic? Is *The Jaguar* a straightforward poem about the one wild animal that is not made listless by captivity? Or does Hughes use the jaguar as a symbol for the poet who is resolved to be himself, while (e.g.) the apes who yawn resemble complacent majorities who have tamely accepted petty irritations (fleas) and the various ways in which modern life imprisons the soul? Is *The Hawk Roosting* (not included in this anthology) a straightforward view of life from the point of view of a predator, or is the hawk a symbol of man's selfish aggressiveness or even of Hitler? One possible answer is that in the early poems Hughes is thinking

literally of an animal or bird whereas in the later poems
(not represented in this anthology) Hughes uses beautiful,
untameable animals and birds as symbols of the passionate
energies in man. In the early poems Hughes is voicing a
powerful sympathy with what he imagines to be the nature
of each beast in *itself*. As time goes on, he grows more self-
consciously aware of what it is that leads him to be
interested in some beasts more than in others. Eventually,
he is writing poems in which the reasons for his interest in a
beast rival in importance his imaginative concept of the
beast's own state of being. His jaguar is very much a jaguar,
but his crow is only incidentally and intermittently a crow.

Another possible answer is that in Hughes' poetry the
literal and the symbolic are enmeshed together. For instance, while *The Thought-Fox* is about a real fox, the
animal's actions also symbolise the poetic process.
Similarly, *An Otter* is about an authentic otter, but the
otter nosing in the water to inspect the 'most secret interior'
of frogs and rotten stumps symbolises the poet collecting
material for his writing. As Ted Hughes wrote:

> There are all sorts of ways of capturing animals and
> birds and fish. I spent most of my time, up to the age of
> fifteen or so trying out many of these ways and when my
> enthusiasm began to wane, as it did gradually, I started
> to write poems .... The two interests have been one
> interest .... In a way, I suppose, I think of poems as a
> sort of animal. They have their own life, like animals.

And Hughes answers our rhetorical question in what he
writes about *The Thought-Fox*: It's about a fox, obviously enough, but a fox that's both a fox and not a
fox.... It is both a fox and a spirit.' Whichever view we
take, we will agree that Hughes' most significant theme
is the central opposition between the vital, instinctive
impulses of birds and animals, often violent and
destructive, and the dulled or tamed consciousness of
over-civilised people or passive animals.

A DREAM OF HORSES

WE were born grooms, in stable-straw we sleep still,
All our wealth horse-dung and the combings of horses,
And all we can talk about is what horses ail.

Out of the night that gulfed beyond the palace-gate
There shook hooves and hooves and hooves of horses:
Our horses battered their stalls; their eyes jerked white.

And we ran out, mice in our pockets and straw in our
    hair,
Into darkness that was avalanching to horses
And a quake of hooves. Our lantern's little orange flare

Made a round mask of our each sleep-dazed face,
Bodiless, or else bodied by horses
That whinnied and bit and cannoned the world from its
    place.

The tall palace was so white, the moon was so round,
Everything else this plunging of horses
To the rim of our eyes that strove for the shapes of the
    sound.

We crouched at our lantern, our bodies drank the din,
And we longed for a death trampled by such horses
As every grain of the earth had hooves and mane.

We must have fallen like drunkards into a dream
Of listening, lulled by the thunder of the horses.   20
We awoke stiff; broad day had come.

Out through the gate the unprinted desert stretched
To stone and scorpion; our stable-horses
Lay in their straw, in a hag-sweat, listless and wretched.

Now let us, tied, be quartered by these poor horses,
If but doomsday's flames be great horses,
The forever itself a circling of the hooves of horses.

THE JAGUAR

THE apes yawn and adore their fleas in the sun.
The parrots shriek as if they were on fire, or strut
Like cheap tarts to attract the stroller with the nut.
Fatigued with indolence, tiger and lion

Lie still as the sun. The boa-constrictor's coil
Is a fossil. Cage after cage seems empty, or
Stinks of sleepers from the breathing straw.
It might be painted on a nursery wall.

But who runs like the rest past these arrives
At a cage where the crowd stands, stares, mesmerized,   10
As a child at a dream, at a jaguar hurrying enraged
Through prison darkness after the drills of his eyes

On a short fierce fuse. Not in boredom —
The eye satisfied to be blind in fire,
By the bang of blood in the brain deaf the ear —
He spins from the bars, but there's no cage to him

More than to the visionary his cell:
His stride is wildernesses of freedom:
The world rolls under the long thrust of his heel.
Over the cage floor the horizons come.   20

THE THOUGHT-FOX

I IMAGINE this midnight moment's forest:
Something else is alive
Beside the clock's loneliness
And this blank page where my fingers move.

Through the window I see no star:
Something more near
Though deeper within darkness
Is entering the loneliness:

Cold, delicately as the dark snow,
A fox's nose touches twig, leaf;   10
Two eyes serve a movement, that now
And again now, and now, and now

Sets neat prints into the snow
Between trees, and warily a lame
Shadow lags by stump and in hollow
Of a body that is bold to come

Across clearings, an eye,
A widening deepening greenness,
Brilliantly, concentratedly,
Coming about its own business   20

Till, with a sudden sharp hot stink of fox
It enters the dark hole of the head.
The window is starless still; the clock ticks,
The page is printed.

WIND

THIS house has been far out at sea all night,
The woods crashing through darkness, the booming hills,
Winds stampeding the fields under the window
Floundering black astride and blinding wet

Till day rose; then under an orange sky
The hills had new places, and wind wielded
Blade-light, luminous black and emerald,
Flexing like the lens of a mad eye.

At noon I scaled along the house-side as far as
The coal-house door. I dared once to look up —   10
Through the brunt wind that dented the balls of my eyes
The tent of the hills drummed and strained its guyrope,

The fields quivering, the skyline a grimace,
At any second to bang and vanish with a flap:
The wind flung a magpie away and a black-
Back gull bent like an iron bar slowly. The house

Rang like some fine green goblet in the note
That any second would shatter it. Now deep
In chairs, in front of the great fire, we grip
Our hearts and cannot entertain book, thought,   20

Or each other. We watch the fire blazing,
And feel the roots of the house move, but sit on,
Seeing the window tremble to come in,
Hearing the stones cry out under the horizons.

A WOMAN UNCONSCIOUS

Russia and America circle each other;
Threats nudge an act that were without doubt
A melting of the mould in the mother,
Stones melting about the root.

The quick of the earth burned out:
The toil of all our ages a loss
With leaf and insect. Yet flitting thought
(Not to be thought ridiculous)

Shies from the world-cancelling black
Of its playing shadow: it has learned   10
That there's no trusting (trusting to luck)
Dates when the world's due to be burned;

That the future's no calamitous change
But a malingering of now,
Histories, towns, faces that no
Malice or accident much derange.

And though bomb be matched against bomb,
Though all mankind wince out and nothing endure —
Earth gone in an instant flare —
Did a lesser death come   20

Onto the white hospital bed
Where one, numb beyond her last of sense,
Closed her eyes on the world's evidence
And into pillows sunk her head.

AN OTTER

I

UNDERWATER eyes, an eel's
Oil of water body, neither fish nor beast is the otter:
  Four-legged yet water-gifted, to outfish fish;
    With webbed feet and long ruddering tail
    And a round head like an old tomcat.

    Brings the legend of himself
From before wars or burials, in spite of hounds and
      vermin-poles;
  Does not take root like the badger. Wanders, cries;
    Gallops along land he no longer belongs to;
    Re-enters the water by melting.   10

    Of neither water nor land. Seeking
Some world lost when first he dived, that he cannot come
      at since,
  Takes his changed body into the holes of lakes;
    As if blind, cleaves the stream's push till he licks
    The pebbles of the source; from sea

    To sea crosses in three nights
Like a king in hiding. Crying to the old shape of the
      starlit land,
  Over sunken farms where the bats go round,
    Without answer. Till light and birdsong come
    Walloping up roads with the milk wagon.   20

II

    The hunt's lost him. Pads on mud,
    Among sedges, nostrils a surface bead,
    The otter remains, hours. The air,
    Circling the globe, tainted and necessary,

Mingling tobacco-smoke, hounds and parsley,
Comes carefully to the sunk lungs.
So the self under the eye lies,
Attendant and withdrawn. The otter belongs

In double robbery and concealment —   29
From water that nourishes and drowns, and from land
That gave him his length and the mouth of the hound.
He keeps fat in the limpid integument

Reflections live on. The heart beats thick,
Big trout muscle out of the dead cold;
Blood is the belly of logic; he will lick
The fishbone bare. And can take stolen hold

On a bitch otter in a field full
Of nervous horses, but linger nowhere.
Yanked above hounds, reverts to nothing at all,
To this long pelt over the back of a chair.   40

THRUSHES

TERRIFYING are the attent sleek thrushes on the lawn,
More coiled steel than living — a poised
Dark deadly eye, those delicate legs
Triggered to stirrings beyond sense — with a start, a
     bounce, a stab
Overtake the instant and drag out some writhing thing.
No indolent procrastinations and no yawning stares,
No sighs or head-scratchings. Nothing but bounce and
     stab
And a ravening second.

Is it their single-mind-sized skulls, or a trained
Body, or genius, or a nestful of brats   10
Gives their days this bullet and automatic

Purpose? Mozart's brain had it, and the shark's mouth
That hungers down the blood-smell even to a leak of its
　　　own
Side and devouring of itself: efficiency which
Strikes too streamlined for any doubt to pluck at it
Or obstruction deflect.

With a man it is otherwise. Heroisms on horseback,
Outstripping his desk-diary at a broad desk,
Carving at a tiny ivory ornament
For years: his act worships itself — while for him,　　20
Though he bends to be blent in the prayer, how loud and
　　　above what
Furious spaces of fire do the distracting devils
Orgy and hosannah, under what wilderness
Of black silent waters weep.

PENNINES IN APRIL

If this county were a sea (that is solid rock
Deeper than any sea) these hills heaving
Out of the east, mass behind mass, at this height
Hoisting heather and stones to the sky
Must burst upwards and topple into Lancashire.

Perhaps, as the earth turns, such ground-stresses
Do come rolling westward through the locked land.
Now, measuring the miles of silence
Your eye takes the strain: through

Landscapes gliding blue as water　　　　　　　10
Those barrellings of strength are heaving slowly and heave
To your feet and surf upwards
In a still, fiery air, hauling the imagination,
Carrying the larks upward.

NOTES

YEATS

TO A SHADE

Yeats's gift for satire was developing in 1913 when this was written. The *Shade* is the ghost of Parnell (1846–91), who was the leader of the Irish M.P.s in the House of Commons until he was repudiated by many of them because he was cited as a co-respondent in a divorce case. Yeats is condemning the Irish for their ingratitude to Parnell, and to Sir Hugh Lane, who offered a collection of French Impressionist paintings to the Dublin Art Gallery on condition that suitable rooms were built to display them. The Dublin public objected to details of Lane's later proposals, such as the choice of an English architect. Later he was so hurt that he lent them to the National Gallery in London. He later wrote an *unwitnessed* codicil to his will leaving the pictures to the Dublin Art Gallery, but before it could be made legal he was drowned when the Germans torpedoed the *Lusitania*. The National Gallery kept the pictures for many years but eventually agreed that they should be exhibited in London and Dublin in turn.

l. 17. **an old foul mouth**: William Martin Murphy, who owned two Dublin newspapers that attacked Parnell and Lane.

l. 18. The Irish are thought of as a pack of hounds attacking a stag.

l. 19. **Glasnevin**: the cemetery where Parnell was buried, in Dublin.

EASTER 1916

On Easter Monday 1916 the Irish rebelled against the English, thinking that it was an opportune moment because the English were so hard pressed by the Germans. The Irish leaders were people whom Yeats knew personally, but he was surprised when they stopped talking about independence and acted so rashly. For some days the rebels held out in the G.P.O. and other important buildings in Dublin, but soon they were captured. The British promptly shot sixteen of the leaders.

Yeats's poem hails the Irish dead as patriotic martyrs, and explores the nature of their heroism. He feels personally involved because his nationalist play, *Cathleen ni Houlihan*, had helped drive them to rebel. His attitude to them is complex; he regrets their deaths, and blames himself for urging them on; he admires the dead heroes' bravery but he fears that all who devote themselves fanatically to the narrow cause of Irish nationalism may find their hearts turned to stone. He ends optimistically, hoping that Easter 1916 may have begun a happier era for Ireland.

l. 13. Being certain: This shows how he underrated them. He was amazed when his friends acted like heroes.

l. 17. That woman: Constance Markiewicz, *née* Gore-Booth, was imprisoned; she was one of the original leaders and would have been shot but for her sex. She was later the first woman elected to the British Parliament though she never took her seat because she was still in prison. Yeats also wrote about her in 'On a Political Prisoner' and 'In memory of Eva Gore-Booth and Con Markiewicz'.

l. 24. This man: Patrick Pearse, an Irish poet and the owner of St. Enda's School, Dublin. He was President of the Irish provisional government in Easter Week. After the Irish in the G.P.O. surrendered, the fifteen leaders who were shot included Patrick Pearse, Thomas MacDonagh, John MacBride and James Connolly. (The sixteenth, Casement, was later hanged.)

l. 26. This other his helper and friend: MacDonagh helped Pearse run the school. His *Literature in Ireland* was an excellent book.

l. 31. This other man: MacBride. The *bitter wrong* to which Yeats refers was to marry Maud Gonne and then to make her so unhappy with his drinking that she was compelled to leave him. In the Easter Rising he led an attack on a factory with great bravery.

ll. 41–56. Those who are enchanted to a stone are those who gave up too many other interests to concentrate too narrowly on a cause. But the image is complex; the stone represents their eternal fame as well as their hardened hearts and inhuman inflexibility.

l. 73. Bewildered: The choice of the verb shows that when Yeats wrote the poem in September 1916 he was very unsure whether the rebellion would succeed and so justify their self-sacrifice.

l. 76. Connolly: a trade-union organiser.

IN MEMORY OF MAJOR ROBERT GREGORY

Major Robert Gregory was the only son of Lady Gregory; he was killed in an air combat over the Italian Front in 1918. Within a few months of his death Yeats wrote both this poem about him and also the shorter poem, 'An Irish Airman Foresees his Death'.

We are allowed to overhear Yeats thinking aloud; he elevates his private sorrow into a public elegy. He mourns Robert Gregory as a successful fighter-pilot, a fine horseman, a scholar, and a gifted painter who had designed scenery for the Abbey Theatre. Yeats admired his confidence and lack of introspection and — most of all — his all-round brilliance; Yeats insisted that he was 'the most accomplished man I have ever known'.

l. 1. **our house:** Thoor Ballylee. A Norman tower in Galway which was still being made fit to move into. Robert Gregory had been consulted about the conversion of it and had completed a remarkable painting of it. Yeats, having married in the previous year, was looking forward to moving into it with his wife; and this elegy arises casually from the house-warming he imagines for it.

l. 13. Newly married couples are apt to quarrel about which of the bridegroom's bachelor friends shall be invited to their new home.

l. 17. *et seq.* He lists three dead friends who had a partial view of the reality which Robert Gregory saw as a whole. Johnson was a scholar, Synge an artist, and George Pollexfen a fine horseman; Robert Gregory was all three. Lionel Johnson (1867–1902) was a scholar and poet whose most famous poem is 'By the Statue of King Charles in Charing Cross'.

l. 19. **much falling:** He developed weaknesses of character, especially drunkenness. His falling from a high stool in a pub is mentioned in Pound's *Hugh Selwyn Mauberley*.

ll. 25–32. The dramatist John Millington Synge (1871–1909) could never have died contentedly if he had not fulfilled himself as a writer, just before his death (i.e. *dying*), by writing about the people of the Aran Islands, who come to life in his plays.

l. 33. **George Pollexfen:** Yeats's uncle, who had been a brilliant horseman, became very interested in magical symbolism and astrology.

l. 47. **Our Sidney:** Sir Philip Sidney, like Major Gregory, was a young man who showed great promise in several arts but was killed fighting abroad. He equalled Major Gregory's versatility because he was an important poet and critic, as well as a brave soldier; even at death's door he reputedly gave up the water to the soldier who needed it more than he did. He was therefore the epitome of all that Johnson, Synge and Pollexfen achieved separately.

ll. 65–66. In describing the scene Yeats is remembering an actual painting of Coole Park by Major Gregory. The clear, rain-laden light reveals purplish grey rocks in the foreground and mountains in the distance.

l. 91. **those that manhood tried:** friends such as Synge.

or (those that) childhood loved: relatives such as Pollexfen.

l. 92. This refers to Lionel Johnson.

SAILING TO BYZANTIUM

Byzantium and Constantinople were two adjacent towns that merged into one city. In 395 the Roman Empire was divided into two, and Byzantium became the capital of the Eastern Empire. It remained the capital of an Empire until the Turks captured it in 1453.

The historic Byzantium was remarkable for the skill of its craftsmen and the beauty of its buildings. But Yeats is writing about an ideal city; Byzantium has become for him a Utopia, a symbol of holiness, of perfect craftsmanship, and of Ireland's future achievement in the arts; it is the world of intellect and spirit as distinct from the world of the senses.

In *A Vision* Yeats explains why he uses Byzantium as his symbol:

> In the fifth century ... Byzantium became Byzantine, and substituted for formal Roman magnificence, with its glorification of physical power, an architecture that suggests the sacred City in the Apocalypse of St. John. I think if I could be given a month of antiquity and leave to spend it where I chose, I would spend it in Byzantium a little before Justinian opened St. Sophia and closed the Academy of Plato. I think I would find in some little wine shop some philosophical worker in mosaic who could answer all my questions, the supernatural descending nearer to him ... for the pride of his delicate skill would make what was an instrument of power to Princes and Clerics and a murderous madness in the mob, show as a lovely flexible presence like that of a perfect human body. I think that in early Byzantium, maybe never before or since in recorded history, religious, aesthetic and practical life were one, and that architect and artificers ... spoke to the multitude and the few alike. The painter, the mosaic worker, the worker in gold and silver, the illuminator of Sacred Books, were almost impersonal, almost perhaps without the consciousness of individual design, absorbed in their subject-matter and that the vision of a whole people.

ll. 1–8. That is the country he is leaving with regret — the Ireland of his youth, the country of young love and physical vitality. He has grown too old to fit into its life.

l. 4. **the salmon-falls:** He is thinking of Sligo. The river drops down through the town in a series of falls up which the salmon leap in the spring when returning to spawn. Salmon are symbols of strength and beauty.

l. 7. **Caught:** The young man is caught up in the sensual music as surely as fish are caught up in a net.

ll. 9–24. Though his body is deteriorating with old age, he is resolved to find compensation by achieving a new perfection of the soul. His soul must clap its hands for joy as it realises it is approaching nearer to perfection; he is thinking of how when William Blake's brother died, Blake had a vision of his brother's soul going up to heaven and clapping its hands for joy. The soul must also 'sing' — an idea which combines the ideas of singing for joy and of writing poetry. To teach his soul to sing he must, metaphorically, sail to Byzantium. The only way in which the soul can learn to *sing* is by studying *monuments of its own magnificence* such as Byzantine art.

Yeats had read Plutarch's idea that the souls of enlightened men return to be schoolmasters of the living, whom they influence unseen. (In l. 13 **but** means *except*.)

l. 17. **God's holy fire:** This image combines several previous ideas. Isaiah (vi. 6) describes how when God wished to inspire him, one of the seraphim touched his lips with a live coal. Plotinus (born A.D. 205) stressed the idea of escaping from the body and the material world. Plate 84 in the illustrations that Blake drew for Dante's poems shows Dante entering the refining Holy Fire. Yeats took many of his images from drawings of Blake that had remained vivid in his memory.

l. 19. **perne in a gyre:** A perne is the spool or bobbin on which thread is spun. Yeats picked up the word when he was a boy and watched the smoke from cotton mills and flour mills near Sligo. The image is of a shuttle revolving round and up the walls of time, in an upward spiral movement, leaving behind it the thread as a clue by which the depths may be explored again.

In several poems, especially 'The Second Coming', he thought of successive ages as a system of gyres, or spirals of predestined events. The gyre is always expanding or contracting; therefore two cones symbolise the double effect of such tensions as are set up by the conflict between the heart and the head. The two cones point in opposite directions, and the apex of one coincides with the base of the other. Within the cone moves the perne, the spool which unwinds the thread that the previous age has wound. As each age reaches its climax at the end of its movement the gyre 'widens' or expands till it disintegrates, and the new age begins to unwind the old thread. (See Chapters 11 and 12, *The Lonely Tower* by T. R. Henn.)

l. 25-32. He believes that once he is dead ('out of nature') his ghost can choose to take any bodily shape. His choice will be an artificial singing-bird made of gold by a Byzantine craftsman. He insists on *gold* because it is a Platonic symbol of perfection.

BYZANTIUM

In this poem Yeats is no longer an uninitiated observer sailing to Byzantium; he is an initiate who views it from inside. But, just as he does in 'Sailing to Byzantium', he again praises the eternity of art in order to stop himself from regretting the decline of his youthful vigour.

ll. 1-8. These lines set the scene, Byzantium about A.D. 500 and midnight. The city, having an artistic architectural unity, disdains man's incoherent moodiness.

l. 1. **images:** As night approaches, the grosser realities of day fade. Day may be a symbol for mortal life, night for life after death.

l. 4. **gong:** A. N. Jeffares in *W. B. Yeats: Man and Poet* points out that

Yeats read the following passage in W. G. Holmes's *The Age of Justinian and Theodora* which describes the boom of the great *semantron*, a sonorous board suspended in the porch of each church and beaten by deacons with wooden mallets or gongs. This midnight gong symbolises the moment of death.

l. 8. **fury:** Creative urge. 'Fury' suggests what is noble in man, as 'Mire' suggests what is ignoble. Plotinus uses *mire* as a symbol for the corruptibility of matter.

ll. 9-16. Yeats imagines that when he dies he will be transported back in time to Byzantium. He will be met by a spirit who will teach him wisdom. This superhuman form — 'shade more than man' — will summon Yeats's spirit, about to be freed from life's inferior qualities and complexity, and reincarnate it.

l. 9. **image:** The shade in a comparatively materialised condition — e.g. a spirit with a visible ghost.

        shade: A spirit that is quite invisible but yet can communicate with certain human beings.

ll. 11-12. The rotation of an ordinary (literal) bobbin unwinds cotton thread. Similarly the rotation of this supernatural bobbin unwinds bands of cloth such as are wrapped round a mummy. These lead one through the labyrinth of life, as Ariadne's thread led Theseus through the Cretan labyrinth: the mummy, as it unwinds its burial cloth, removes all that is evil or inferior and leaves behind the purified spirit. This *Hades bobbin* was once a man, but now it is a purified spirit that has peeled off its human incarnations as a mummy might peel off its wrappings.

l. 14. **Breathless:** dead.

ll. 17-24. The purified soul becomes a golden singing-bird, permanent and spiritual, that scorns all human characteristics. The goldsmith's art is permanent, or at least is a symbol of permanence. The mosaics depict spiritual experience. The technique of the goldsmiths and of the artists who created the mosaics have triumphed over the limitations of the body — over *the fury and the mire of human veins*.

l. 19. As in l. 5. Yeats considers starlight more constant than moonlight.

l. 21. **embittered:** T. R. Henn in *The Lonely Tower* suggests that *the moon — symbol of womanhood and of flux or instability — leaves it* 'embittered' *in the light which shines pale on the gold. The cock, the dominant untiring male, is* 'embittered', *scorned by the moon.*

l. 23. **common bird:** An ordinary, mortal, short-lived bird. Yeats considers the artificial golden bird much nearer to the ideal bird in Heaven than any mortal nightingale is. Sturge Moore had criticised 'Sailing to Byzantium' because its goldsmith's bird was too natural; Yeats took the criticism seriously and here explicitly describes the bird as superior to any natural bird.

ll. 25-40. The time of the poem is confined to that marked by the twelve strokes of midnight which is thought of as the moment of death. As the clock strikes, the flames, painted in a mosaic on the Emperor's floor, spring to life; they are nearer to the ideal than ordinary flames and they purify any newly arrived spirits, formerly 'blood-begotten', which have been ferried to Byzantium over the sea of time and space by rescuing dolphins. The dance purifies because it breaks the cycles or gyres, and so rescues the soul from the predestined pattern of birth, death and reincarnation in which we are trapped. The mosaics give permanence to a spiritual experience and so the spirit triumphs over the body (mere mire and blood) and Byzantium acts as a city of regeneration.

ll. 36–37. The mosaics on the floor, where ritual dances were held, break the cycle in which the spirit is born and reborn in successive reincarnations. They impose a pattern on complex, irrational, confused things, and put an end to the sources of confusion.

l. 40. **dolphin-torn:** as the dolphins ferry the dead across the sea of life, they tear the surface of the waves. They also represent sensual existence.

gong-tormented: the gong strikes the midnight hour and is therefore a reminder of the moment of death. The sea of life is tormented with the idea of death.

THE TOWER

During the years 1917–18 the castle which Yeats had bought at Thoor Ballylee in Western Ireland, near to Lady Gregory's stately home at Coole, was modernised and made habitable. The tower was more than a building: it was a symbol of the poet's isolation, and of his resolve to lead a lonely life of wisdom; since it contained a spiral staircase, it was also related in his mind to the image of a gyre. At the same time, we are meant to think of Shelley's visionary Prince Athanase, who was clothed in love and justice —

> *In which he sate*
> *Apart from men as in a lonely tower —*

and of the melancholy scholar in Milton's 'Il Penseroso' —

> *Or let my lamp at midnight hour*
> *Be seen in some high lonely tower.*

Since Ireland is full of old towers, the tower links him with Ireland's past; and since it dominates the countryside around, it is a symbol of the aristocracy. The people mentioned in the poem had lived in the locality. Mrs. French lived there in the eighteenth century. The peasant beauty was named Mary Hynes and the blind poet was Anthony Raftery (1784–1834). In Yeats's early poem, 'Stories of Red Hanrahan', he creates the character of Hanrahan, who pursued the phantom hare and hounds. Yeats believed that ghosts had been seen playing dice in the room that became his bedroom. The old bankrupt man lived about 1800: he could only leave the Castle on a Sunday because of his creditors.

Yeats was fifty-three when he wrote the poem: he felt that he had to come to terms with old age, and find compensation for his bodily decline in the search for intellectual interests.

l. 12. **Plato and Plotinus:** Plato (427–347 B.C.) was the great Athenian philosopher. Plotinus (A.D. 205–270), a Greek philosopher born in Egypt, thought that the soul detests being in the body, and therefore he advocated asceticism. He believed that this led to moments of ecstatic vision of the highest good.

l. 33. *et seq.* As Yeats writes of Mary Hynes, she and Helen of Troy and Maude Gonne have almost become one person in his mind.

l. 65. **bawn:** fortified enclosure.

l. 79. **his dog's day:** Hamlet says *The cat will mew and dog will have his day.*

l. 85. **the Great Memory:** Yeats believed that the corporate memory of the race remembered images and symbols that had meant a lot to people in the past.

l. 90. **half-mounted:** Describes the bankrupt. The gentry were mounted men: a mere squire was a half-mounted man.

l. 105. **Old lecher:** Hanrahan.

l. 114. **woman lost:** Maud Gonne.

l. 132. **Burke and Grattan:** Edmund Burke (1729–97) was an Irishman who took a leading part in English political life from 1765 (when he became secretary to a Whig leader, Rockingham), till his death. Grattan (1746–1820) played a leading part in the semi-independent Irish Parliament, 1782–1801. They stand for a period when aristocratic leadership was acquiring for Ireland a reasonable degree of independence.

l. 140. The swan is a complex symbol of the bird that sings as it dies, of a civilisation that is passing, and of Jupiter's courtship of Leda.

l. 146. **I mock Plotinus' thought:** Is it illogical to *choose Plato and Plotinus for a friend* (l. 12) and yet now to *mock Plotinus' thought and cry in Plato's teeth*? To excuse this apparent contradiction Yeats put forward the view that the Platonic ideal archetypes existed, but had been created by man's own thought: once they had been created, they retained an independent existence, and so became 'superhuman' (l. 164).

l. 165. **mirror-resembling dream:** This dream is the invention of man which shapes the future — *the image-making power of the mind.* As birds draw on the Great Memory — the *Anima Mundi* — to build their nests, so men draw on the poet's imaginings (cf. Eliot: *These fragments I have shored against my ruins*). Yeats was deeply interested in studying how birds in captivity retained the instinct to create their nests in conformity with the race-pattern. He experimented with his canaries — at the very time when he was writing this poem — and he related their instinctive behaviour to his concept of the Great Memory. He was delighted to find evidence in Nature for his beliefs. This image in l. 165 thus has a vital connexion with the first part of the poem — that the men of the past in Ireland have bequeathed their pride to the modern Irish, as though they had left it in their wills. In the same way Yeats will bequeath his faith and pride to later generations; so he can face death with equanimity, because like the birds he can pass on his skills to his descendants. The bird-imagery is, therefore, an essential part of the logical content of the poem.

l. 166. **As at the loophole there:** The poet builds his poems as instinctively (undeliberately yet skilfully) as the jackdaws build their nests.

l. 194. **a bird's sleepy cry:** Yeats will accept death as naturally as the jackdaw accepts nightfall — after one last sleepy caw, it settles to rest.

THE WILD SWANS AT COOLE

Coole Park was the ancestral house and estate which Lady Gregory's husband's family had owned since the eighteenth century.

In October 1916, Yeats looks at the swans on the lake and imagines that they are the same swans as he counted in 1897; they certainly show no signs of age or change, while he has grown very noticeably older. He is fifty-one instead of thirty-two. Maud Gonne has refused him in 1916 just as she did in 1897.

COOLE PARK 1929

In this poem Yeats regrets the decline of the aristocratic life that was coming to an end.

l. 2. **an aged woman and her house:** Lady Gregory sold Coole Park to the Forestry Department, who allowed her to live in it as a tenant till her death. They sold it and it was eventually demolished, as Yeats foretells in the last stanza, though the gardens remained in existence.

l. 9. **Hyde:** Douglas Hyde (1860–1949) was a poet who became the first President of Eire.

l. 11. **one that ruffled in a manly pose:** Yeats himself.

l. 14. **Shawe-Taylor and Hugh Lane:** Lady Gregory's nephews, who were dead. Hugh Lane was referred to in 'To A Shade'.

l. 17. **swallows:** Visitors usually came to Coole only in summer.

l. 24. **withershins:** anti-clockwise, and therefore in an unlucky direction.

ll. 25–34. Re-assembling his characters, he foretells the destruction of the house, but imagines the ghosts of his friends meeting again to pay a tribute to Lady Gregory.

COOLE AND BALLYLEE, 1931

Ballylee: the locality of Yeats's Tower. It was once part of the Coole estate, to which it was linked by a river that flowed past the Tower, disappeared underground, re-emerged in Coole demesne and flowed into the lake. In this poem Yeats regrets the imminent death of Lady Gregory and the imminent destruction of her beautiful house, also of the aristocratic virtues ('traditional sanctity and loveliness') that such great houses preserved.

l. 4. **Raftery:** Anthony Raftery (1784–1834), the blind Gaelic poet, called the part where the river flows underground 'The Cellar'. He is referred to in 'The Tower'.

l. 8. **What's water but the generated soul?** The swan and water are emblems of the soul and inspiration. Just as the river flows underground and then rises, so the soul progresses out of light (life) into the darkness of death, and is then re-incarnated.

l. 12. **buskin:** high leather boots worn by Greek actors when acting in tragedy.

l. 14. **the mounting swan:** a symbol of inspiration.

ll. 17–24. The swan postpones Yeats's tragic mood until the later stanzas. Yeats presents two opposed images for the soul, the water and the swan.

l. 25. **stick:** The aged Lady Gregory uses a walking-stick.

l. 30. **a last inheritor:** her only son was Major Robert Gregory, killed in action.

l. 39. **We shift about:** We rootless inhabitants of a modern town keep changing our house, and keep changing our minds, unlike the aristocratic families who lived in the same house and maintained the same values for centuries.

l. 41. **We were the last romantics:** He is thinking of Synge, Gogarty, George Russell (A.E.) and himself, i.e. of the greater and wiser people with whom he formerly mixed when Lady Gregory's house was full of the best people in Ireland.

l. 46. **that high horse riderless:** Pegasus.

l. 48. **Where the swan drifts:** The final line is sinister and tragic. The swan is a symbol of strength, purity, immortality and — because of the legendary beauty of its last song — it is a symbol of the ecstasy of death.

BEFORE THE WORLD WAS MADE

Yeats is thinking of Plato's idea of Archetypes. Plato believed that every object on earth was an imperfect copy of the ideal Archetype in heaven: for instance, a tree is an imperfect copy of an ideal tree in heaven; a tree painted by an artist or described by a poet is an

imperfect copy of an imperfect copy — twice removed from the ideal.
Rupert Brooke wrote these lines about the Platonic heaven:

> There the Eternals are, and there
> The Good, the Lovely and the True,
> And Types, whose earthly copies were
> The Foolish broken things we knew.

Yeats uses this idea in his poetry, but adapts it. In the two poems
about Byzantium he considers the artificial bird made by the craftsman as superior to any natural bird, and so nearer to the ideal bird in
heaven. In this poem he thinks of the girl making up her face as an
idealist, striving to make her face more similar to the Archetype of a
woman's face that attains perfection in heaven.

LAPIS LAZULI

Lapis lazuli is a semi-precious blue stone, and Yeats possessed a piece
of it carved in the way that he describes in ll. 37-56.

ll. 1-2. Yeats is thinking both of women whom he knew before 1916
who grew too narrowly devoted to political causes and underrated
the arts (*the palette and fiddle-bow*) and also of women in the 1930's
who wanted to devote all their energies to resisting Hitler and
other Fascists.

l. 7. **bomb-balls:** A bomb is a hollow iron ball filled with explosive
and exploded by a fuse or by the force of the impact when it is
dropped or thrown or fired. The technical term is appropriate,
therefore, to both the missiles fired by the cannon of William III
and those which Hitler's planes were threatening to drop. Yeats is
discussing the role of the artist in a world threatened by modern
war.

ll. 9-24. Lear and Hamlet are about to die, but they are still great
and exultant in the face of death. We must be as unafraid of death
as they are.

ll. 25-36. Yeats reminds us that other civilisations have fallen, and
that we should not feel too sorry for ourselves if our civilisation
suffers the same fate. Callimachus was an Athenian sculptor,
living about 450 B.C., who perfected the Corinthian column.

ll. 37-56. Yeats describes the three Chinamen carved out of his piece
of lapis lazuli. They signify the perfection of art, and he urges us
to behave in our bomb-threatened lives with the dignity of
people in art — whether they are Hamlet on the stage or three
Chinamen in a carving.

WHY SHOULD NOT OLD MEN BE MAD?

l. 1. **mad:** Yeats puns on the two meanings of the word — angry
and insane.

l. 3. **a sound fly-fisher's wrist:** He uses the fisherman often as a symbol of the ideal man who is a cultured man of action.

l. 5. **a girl that knew all Dante:** He is thinking of Iseult, Maud Gonne's daughter.

l. 7. **A Helen:** Yeats remembers that Miss Horniman, who helped finance the Abbey Theatre, had feared that Maud Gonne would persuade him to turn his plays and poems into propaganda; she had once told Yeats: *The greatest poet is always helpless beside a beautiful woman screaming from a cart.* But it seems to have been Con MarKiewicz who made speeches from a cart.

THE CIRCUS ANIMALS' DESERTION

The title means that Yeats is deserted by new themes for his poetry.

ll. 1-2. repeat the idea of the title.

ll. 3-8. Therefore he looks back on some of the themes of the poetry he had already written. He sees the thoughts and images of his previous poems as a long circus train, including circus animals, boys on stilts (compare the *high horse* which Homer rode, in 'Coole and Ballylee', 1931), a lion with its woman lion-tamer, and a burnished chariot; they are all controlled by the poet-ringmaster.

ll. 9-16. Failing to think of a new theme, he makes poetry of his barrenness. He finds consolation in enumerating old themes; and he goes on to think about the relationship between his own life and that of the fictitious characters whom he had created. His first example is Oisin, the Gaelic hero of 'The Wanderings of Oisin' (1889), who was captivated by Niamh as completely as Yeats was by Maud Gonne.

l. 11. Yeats explained the three islands visited by Oisin as representing *infinite feeling, infinite battle, infinite repose.*

ll. 17-22. His next example is his play *The Countess Cathleen,* whose heroine is a projection of Maud Gonne.

ll. 19-24. Maud Gonne turned into a political fanatic; this and the writing of his nationalist plays led Yeats into his dream of founding an Irish National Theatre, which he and Lady Gregory partly realised when they worked so hard for the Abbey Theatre.

ll. 23-24. **a dream:** Although he began to write *The Countess Cathleen* as a way of expressing his love for Maud Gonne, in the end the *dream* (the technical problem of writing and producing the play) came to dominate his thoughts more than she did.

ll. 25-26. Several of Yeats's poems, and five of his plays — written at dates ranging from 1903 to 1939 — refer to the hero of several Gaelic legends, Cuchulain. He unwittingly killed his son, as Rustum did, and he suffered from moods of blind despair and rage in which he used to fight against the waves of the sea. Whereas in the sagas Cuchulain dies when only middle-aged, Yeats changes the story so that Cuchulain is an old man when he is beheaded by the Blind Man. Cuchulain says of the Fool that he would know everything if he were capable of knowing anything.

Yeats changes the story so as to make closer the parallelism between Cuchulain and himself. Various women desert Cuchulain, just as the circus animals desert Yeats; only Emer, Cuchulain's wife, does not desert him, just as Yeats is left with only his *heart* (l. 40) and his wife.

ll. 29–30. These lines sum up Yeats's habit of seeing someone in a characteristic pose.

l. 33–34. Yeats asks from where he derived his 'masterful images'. He decides that he has derived them from physical existence, from the 'foul rag-and-bone shop' of his own heart.

WILFRED OWEN

SPRING OFFENSIVE

The impact of this poem comes from a series of antitheses, beginning with the contrast between the natural appearance of the grassy slope where the soldiers have to wait, and the unnatural hail of fire to which they are exposed as soon as they attack. One of Owen's technical problems was how to use his gift for romantic description. Here he finds a brilliant use for it in ll. 7–8 and 14–15 to underline this first antithesis.

ll. 4–7. Owen stresses how tense and apprehensive the soldiers are.

l. 15. **slow** (boots): The epithet emphasises how reluctant the soldiers are to leave this comfortable grassland protected by a ridge.

ll. 27–29. The tempo of the poem changes, and the series of short light-sounding words suggests the rapid dart forward of the soldiers, until the heavy stop after 'Exposed' suggests the sudden failure of their attack as the German counter-fire bursts upon them.

l. 37. **Some say God caught them:** In this mood Owen cannot make up his mind about Christianity.

GREATER LOVE

The title refers forcibly to St. John XV. 13: *Greater love hath no man than this, that a man lay down his life for his friends.*

A letter which Owen wrote to his mother from a hospital on the Somme expresses the creed which his poems proclaim:

Already I have comprehended a light which never will filter into

the dogma of any national church: namely, that one of Christ's
essential commands was: Passivity at any price! Suffer dishonour
and disgrace, but never resort to arms. Be bullied, be outraged, be
killed; but do not kill. It may be a chimerical and an ignominious
principle, but there it is. It can only be ignored: and I think pulpit
professionals are ignoring it very skilfully and successfully indeed. . . .
Am I not myself a conscientious objector with a very seared
conscience? . . . Christ is literally in 'No Man's Land'. There men
often hear his voice: Greater love hath no man than this, that a
man lay down his life for a friend. Is it spoken in English only and
French? I do not believe so. Thus you see how pure Christianity
will not fit in with pure patriotism.

10. **Where God seems not to care:** Like Job, Owen had been
   brought up to have a strong religious faith, but he could not
   understand how a good God could allow so much undeserved
   suffering to occur. He chooses the word *seems* to express his
   bewilderment.

ANTHEM FOR DOOMED YOUTH

The sestet seems probably too obvious an imitation of Keats, but there
is some artistic advantage in having a sharp contrast between the two
halves of the poem.

Since Owen scribbled repeated versions of his poems on scraps of
paper or in letters, and never lived to see most of them published, it is
not always certain which version of a particular line Owen would
have ultimately preferred; sometimes we have a fascinating record of
how Owen improved a line immeasurably after trying out perhaps
twenty variants of it. Siegfried Sassoon (1920), Edmund Blunden
(1931) and C. Day Lewis (1963) edited valuable editions of Owen's
poems. Originally this poem was called 'Anthem for Dead Youth' and
began: *What passing-bells for you who died in herds?* But the line that
gave Owen most difficulty was l. 13. Finally Owen presented Sassoon
with a version that bracketed two alternatives, *silent* and *sweet white*.
The second alternative has been scored out; it is too reminiscent of
Masefield's *sweet white wine* and of Keats in his effeminate mood. Later
either Owen or Sassoon pencilled in *patient*, which carries on the
alliteration, but does not contrast with the noises of the octave.

INSENSIBILITY

ll. 1–2. Owen cannot forgive civilians for lacking pity, but he can
   forgive those who are going to be killed themselves in the front
   line if *they* lose any sense of pity for their comrades. But Owen
   regards insensibility as the worst of evils, and so there is complicated irony in *happy* (l. 1).

l. 3. **fleers:** mocks.

ll. 50–59. The poem ends with a burning protest against civilian dullards who are *immune to pity*.

FUTILITY

l. 1. **him**: Owen is writing an epitaph for The Unknown Soldier, for any or every soldier who dies.

l. 3. **fields unsown**: They are symbolic of the promise of youth that he has not had the opportunity to fulfil.

l. 7. **The kind old sun**: Owen pretends to be sentimental before completing the bitterness of his full statement.

ll. 12–14. Again Owen asks why all this suffering had to be. In a century of world wars, mass slaughters and totalitarian governments, Owen asserts that the individual matters; that is why this soldier's death is a tragedy.

AT A CALVARY NEAR THE ANCRE

The Ancre is a tributary of the Somme, joining it near Amiens. A *Calvary* is a representation of the crucifixion such as it is usual to find at a crossroads in France. *Calvary* is also the name which St. Luke's gospel gives to the place where Christ was crucified, though the other gospels call it *Golgotha*.

Owen argues that the Christian churches have done as much damage to Christ's cause by approving of war, as gunfire has done to this statue of Him. The soldier who dies, ordered to fight by his priests and rulers, is thought of as similar to Christ, whose death was brought about by the promptings of the chief priests and the elders.

l. 7. **the Beast**: AntiChrist, as described in Revelations xiii.

INSPECTION

This poem is included as an example of the satirical poems that Owen wrote in a mood more typical of Sassoon than of himself.

ll. 1–8. The rhyme allows Owen to be convincingly colloquial without being unpoetic, and without making the transition to the more dignified lines (ll. 9–16) too abrupt.

l. 7. **damnèd spot**: When Lady Macbeth walks in her sleep, she rubs her hands, which she thinks are still stained with Duncan's blood, and exclaims: 'Out, damnèd spot!'

ll. 15–16. When a field-marshal visits an army unit, it is usual for the officers to compel the men to do such pointless things as whitewashing the coal, so that he will see the camp in an unnatural state of tidiness. With grim irony Owen accuses the churches and governments of *whitewashing* young men by sending them to lose their blood in battle; thus they are made fit to be inspected. Governments and churches regard God as a field-marshal who can easily be deceived.

EXPOSURE

l. 1. **Our brains ache:** an ironic echo of Keats's *Ode to a Nightingale*, which begins: *My heart aches.*

l. 3. **salient:** An outward bulge in the line of trenches. The side holding it would cling grimly to it in hopes of making it a base for a later attack. Since the enemy could fire at it from three sides, its defence usually cost more lives than it was worth.

l. 26. **glozed:** shining, bright.

ll. 26-30. These lines describing the soldier's daydream of a fireside at home are very reminiscent of Keats in style.

ll. 31-32. Here Owen argues that it is a terrible but unavoidable duty to fight in a just war. These lines contradict the passages of complete pacifism that occur in some of his letters.

l. 40. **nothing happens:** On one level of meaning Owen is ironically mimicking the sort of bulletin that a journalist or a general would issue to describe such a day — 'All quiet on the western front'. For a humanist like Owen it is not a day on which *nothing happens* when some men are killed for the burying-party to inter in the frosty ground at night. Yet nothing happens in the sense that mankind is no nearer finding a way of ending the war.

STRANGE MEETING

In the early lines Owen uses a new type of assonance to suggest the noises of battle that penetrate even the tunnel of his dream. There is an echo between *granites* and *titanic* in l. 3 and *distressful* and *bless* in l. 8 etc.

l. 3. **titanic:** Titans were a race of giants who were conquered and supplanted by the later gods led by Zeus or Jupiter.

    groined: Groins are edges made by the intersection of two vaults.

l. 19. **braided:** bound by ribbon.

ll. 26-30. A remarkable prophecy of the movement of European history 1918-39, especially when one remembers that the lines are spoken by a German.

l. 36. This appears to be a deliberate ironic echo of the last line of Wordsworth's 'Ode on The Intimations of Immortality': *Thoughts that do often lie too deep for tears.*

T. S. ELIOT

WHISPERS OF IMMORTALITY

John Webster (1575-1624) wrote tragedies such as *The White Devil* and *The Duchess of Malfi* which express a melancholy attitude to life. For instance, one of his major characters says:

Pleasure of life, what is't?
Only the good hours of an ague.

John Donne (1573–1631) made death a major topic both in his poems and in his sermons (delivered after he became Dean of St. Paul's). In his poem 'The Relique' he imagines the grave-digger opening up his grave, to make room for another corpse, and finding on his wrist

A bracelet of bright hair about the bone.

In a famous passage in a sermon he tells anyone who hears the passing bell: *Ask not for whom the bell tolls. It tolls for thee.* The argument is that when someone else dies, a part of our life dies too.

This poem of Eliot is partly a protest against the shallow outlook which puts too high a value on sexual pleasure such as Grishkin affords. There is meant to be both a parallelism and a contrast between the two halves of the poem, each consisting of four verses.

Webster's vision of the skull beneath the skin is paralleled by the lines which Grishkin has drawn under her eyes: *the breastless creatures underground* are contrasted with the well-developed Grishkin's *friendly bust.* Grishkin's concentration on carnal pleasures is contrasted with the intense thoughtfulness of Webster and Donne, whose ideas about death were so sensitive that they almost became physical sensations.

Eliot does not seem to have thought Webster and Donne *too* much obsessed with death. A phrase such as *expert beyond experience* reveals admiration, and in his critical essays Eliot speaks highly of both writers.

l. 22. **Compels the scampering marmoset:** The smell of the jaguar leaves the marmoset paralysed with fright; similarly Grishkin's charm hypnotises her victims.

ll. 31–32. The **dry ribs** are those of a skeleton. Philosophers are aware of death; it stimulates their thoughts about metaphysics.

In *A Reader's Guide to T. S. Eliot*, George Williamson explains the point of the poem in this way:

> Possessed by death, Webster and Donne saw beyond the flesh: possessed by flesh, we take refuge in abstractions to conceive any life beyond the physical. The challenge of Grishkin or the flesh to such ideas is the problem common to both parts and the problem is not solved by the dry ribs of abstraction. Unlike Webster and Donne, we have to separate thought and sense; otherwise living sense would conquer our feeble metaphysics. Our attitude gives us 'whispers of im-mortality', for they are only the furtive rustling of dry bones.

Grishkin is a body without a mind; abstract entities are minds without bodies.

SWEENEY AMONG THE NIGHTINGALES

Sweeney, the man with an ape's neck, represents all that is primitive and uncultured in modern man. An attempt to seduce (and perhaps kill) him in a café is compared to the murder of Agamemnon whose dying cry, *Ay me! I am smitten with a mortal blow*, provides the epigraph of the poem.

ll. 5–8. The opening stanzas evoke an atmosphere of foreboding. The Raven is a constellation; the Horned Gate is the one through which true dreams pass in Book VI of the *Aeneid*: Dryden translates the relevant lines thus:

> *Two gates the silent house of Sleep adorn;*
> *Of polished ivory this, that of transparent horn.*
> *True visions through transparent horn arise;*
> *Through polished ivory pass deluding lies.*

l. 9. **Gloomy Orion and the Dog:** These are fertility symbols. The constellation of Orion and the Dog star, Sirius, indicated to the ancient Egyptians — by changes in their position — the beginning of the grape harvest and the annual Nile floods respectively. Sweeney would not welcome any symbol of fertility or of a positive faith, just as Rachel denies fertility when she commits the unnatural act of tearing at the grapes. In *The Waste Land* Eliot makes similar use of the fertility symbols of ancient peoples which he had been reading about in Frazer's book *The Golden Bough*.

The Egyptians used to display, on couches, statues of Venus, the Goddess of Love, and of Adonis, the young man who spurned her advances and was killed by a wild boar. Beside the images they placed ripe grapes. The waiter, who offers oranges, bananas, figs, and hothouse grapes to Rachel, is a debased counterpart of an Egyptian offering grapes to Venus.

If *Orion and the Dog are veiled*: this means that the season of fertility is still distant.

l. 17. **The silent man:** Sweeney.

l. 35. **The nightingales:** They sing about adultery, about betrayal and death, about the decay of fertility, about events that resemble those in the Greek myth of Philomela, the woman who was turned into a nightingale. Eliot deliberately uses the nightingales in an unromantic way. Presumably, the convent, in whose gardens they sing, just happens to be opposite the café where Sweeney's death is attempted.

l. 38. **Agamemnon:** When Agamemnon, leader of the Greek armies, returned home after the sack of Troy, he was murdered by his unfaithful wife, Clytaemnestra, and by her lover, Aegisthus. The people in Eliot's poem degrade the natural passion of love, just as the characters in the Greek story did. At the same time, there is a contrast between the Greek myth (described in rhetorical, stylised lines) and modern futility (described in the unheroic rhythms of modern speech). But the full complexity of the poem includes the creation of some sympathy for Sweeney: however much we disapprove of Sweeney's and Agamemnon's faults, we must regard a plot to kill either as a human tragedy.

THE DRY SALVAGES

This is one of a group of four poems called *Four Quartets*, Eliot is transferring to poetry some of the techniques of music, such as dividing the poem into five movements and returning, in a later movement, to themes heard previously. All the individual poems use place-names as their titles; 'The Dry Salvages' (a corruption of *Les Trois Sauvages*) are a group of rocks off the coast of Massachusetts, and the sea-imagery is that of the same coast. However, Eliot does not write poetry about the four places, but about the ideas that the four places suggest to him. (*Salvages* rhymes with *assuages*.)

Eliot's technique in *Four Quartets* presents fewer difficulties for the reader than his earlier technique did. He includes the transitional passages that his earlier poems omitted, and develops a conversational tone suitable for them.

Eliot has developed a metre which makes realistic use of contemporary speech rhythms and avoids the echoes of previous poets that make iambic pentameters seem too 'poetic'. He has succeeded in his search for *a new form of verse which shall be as satisfactory a vehicle for us as blank verse was for the Elizabethans. (A Dialogue of Dramatic Poetry)*. His usual line has four stresses; the number of syllables is unimportant and the great advantage of the new line is its rhythmic flexibility. For instance, ll. 11–14 of *The Dry Salvages* can be analysed in this way:

> His rhythm was present || in the nursery bedroom,
>
> In the rank ailanthus || of the April dooryard,
>
> In the smell of grapes || on the autumn table,
>
> And the evening circle || in the winter gaslight.

Other lines, such as the first two and the last eighteen of the poem, have a different number of stresses per line, but retain the same type of metre.

I

Each quartet has an opening movement in a meditative style which consists of statement and counter-statement; in this poem ll. 1–15 study the history of man's attitude to rivers (e.g. the Mississippi). The movement then goes on to a vision of plenitude: to the river the sea represents plenitude because it is its final destination and because its changelessness makes it independent of time. Clock time is thought of as a driving power that distracts us from our true timeless purpose as God's creatures. The flow of the river symbolises the time we feel in our pulses or in our lives; the sea represents the time that we become intellectually aware of, through a study of history.

l. 5. The builders of bridges, who forget that rivers flood, symbolise men who worship machines and forget God.

ll. 11–14. Eliot is thinking of his childhood when he lived beside the Mississippi.

l. 12. **ailanthus:** an East Indian tree introduced into America.

ll. 15–48. The sea is a symbol of plenitude and also of a second kind of time. But it is also a topic in its own right; Eliot thinks of the various types of terror and waste caused by the sea, until finally he hears the bell on the rocks, The Dry Salvages, to warn sailors.

l. 15. **us:** The *we* of the poem refers to an anonymous crowd of ordinary people such as fishermen, passengers on trains and liners, and worried mothers anxious for their sailor sons.

l. 21. **algae:** seaweed.

l. 44. **before the morning watch:** The Prayer Book translates Psalm 130. 6 thus: *My soul fleeth unto the Lord: before the morning watch, I say, before the morning watch.*

l. 48. The various sinister sounds produced by the sea eventually lead him to concentrate on one sound — the bell-buoy on the dangerous rocks ringing its warning. Later in the poem this is going to remind Eliot of the Angelus bell that summons us to pray to the Virgin.

II

In each quartet the second movement is divided into two parts; the first is a formal lyric, whereas the second, which is meditative, uses a deliberately prosaic rhythm and conversational style.

The rhyme-scheme of the first part is that of a sestina; the same six rhymes are used in each stanza. The rhyming-words of each first five lines (e.g. *wreckage*) suggest negative, despairing ideas of disintegration. But each sixth line ends with a word such as *annunciation*, which expresses a positive hope. The Annunciation was the joyful moment when the Angel announced to the Blessed Virgin Mary that she was to be the mother of Jesus. It was, therefore, the moment in time when Jesus was conceived and began his human existence; it was the moment when God's presence, normally independent of time, descended into time.

The mood of the opening lines is that of Psalm 130, *De Profundis: Out of the deep have I called unto thee, O Lord!* But beneath the apparent despair there is the less obvious theme of faith that prepares us for the ideal of Christ's Annunciation which is going to be emphasised later. A series of annunciations of terror and danger to ordinary mortals leads up to the Angel's joyful Annunciation to the Blessed Virgin Mary.

The opening of the second movement stresses that time is a process of change and decay, but the later part points to different factors which hint at the existence of timeless eternity.

The movement ends by returning to, and re-developing, the river imagery in the first movement.

The ideas of the first lyrical part are translated in the second part into the everyday idioms of ordinary contemporary life. Our past is a part of us that we cannot disown.

The words *beginning* and *end* are deliberately repeated throughout *Four Quartets*, e.g. in ll. 46, 49 and 53. *East Coker* begins:

> *In my beginning is my end.*

ll. 87. *et seq.* Eliot does not believe the common, optimistic view that man is progressing and improving. Many who hold this view quote Darwin's theory of evolution as supporting their arguments.

l. 117. **The bitter apple:** This is an allusion to the Fall.

l. 118. **rock:** a symbol of the eternal truths and virtues that defy time.

III

In each quartet the third movement is an account of movement: it tends to be meditative in its theme and prosaic in its style.

In this particular third movement Eliot now turns to the future, and expresses its relationship to the past, by means of a reference to the religious literature of the Hindus: Arjuna is about to attack a related tribe when he is stopped by the words of Krishna, his charioteer, who is an incarnation of Vishnu, the preserver god. Krishna said that if we are to attain salvation through dutiful action, then that action must be free from the effects of personal desires or interests. To attain this freedom we must attain that state of disinterested detachment which is like leaving the body and the world. We must not take too much thought for the future. In the second part, beginning at l. 132, the railway train that has been a symbol in other quartets reappears. As Helen Gardner says in *The Art of T. S. Eliot*:

> The oppression of the first two poems has lifted. First in a train, then on the ocean, the travellers fare forward, bearing their past with them and their future also. In a real sense they are between two lives; yet to divide time harshly, into past, present and future, is to divide ourselves, to disintegrate personality. . . .
>
> Personality has meaning only in the present, in what we are. Our destination is here; where we are going is where we are.

Time is no healer, because time changes the patient too. When we are on a journey we can forget the past and the future, but this oblivion is an illusion for we change during the journey. According to Krishna our destination is the object that we can contemplate without self-interest.

IV

Each fourth movement is lyrical. The *angelus* is the bell which calls
Roman Catholics at morning, noon and sunset to say prayers in
commemoration of Christ's Incarnation. We are reminded of the bell
ringing at the end of the second movement and of the dangerous
voyages referred to there, and we are prepared for Eliot's meditation
on the Incarnation in the fifth movement.

The reference to the women who have anxiously watched their
husbands sail away reminds us of the women and fishermen previously
referred to in ll. 39–45.

The last two words remind us of the Angel's message to the Virgin
Mary: this also prepared us for the theme of Christ's Incarnation in
the fifth movement.

l. 177. **Figlia del tuo figlio:** 'daughter of your own son' — the
    words with which Dante in *Paradiso* addresses the Mother of
    Jesus.

V

Each fifth movement contains an intricate reworking of themes
suggested previously. This one begins with a list of man's superstitious
ways of foretelling the future; a preoccupation with them is evidence
of a person's lack of genuine religion. To *haruspicate* (l. 186) is to do
this, as Romans did, by studying the entrails of a sacrificed beast. To
scry is to use a crystal in crystal-gazing. Pentagrams (l. 201) were
five-pointed stars used as mystic symbols. Eliot disposes of these
unChristian delusions before arguing that in order to act rightly in the
present we must be free from selfish, anxious calculation about the
future; he goes on to meditate about the Incarnation, which is *The
point of intersection of the timeless with time.* Two planes of being inter-
sected — the timeless life of God and the life of Christ in this time-
dominated world.

The poem ends with the theme of our absorption in the identity of
the Christian Church and the Christian life. The last section of the
poem is thus a profound statement of Eliot's religious conviction. He
recommends a society where both rulers and people humbly merge
their identity with God's.

l. 190. **sortilege:** divination by casting lots.

l. 223. **chthonic:** dwelling beneath the earth.

ll. 226. *et seq. For most of us.* . . .

The poem is not about saints with unusual gifts but about the fears
of ordinary people and their occasional glimpse of religious truth.
These glimpses must not be relied on but must be received with
gratitude to God when they do occur.

l. 232. **the yew-tree:** represents burial in the familiar comforting
    surroundings of a country churchyard.

JOHN BETJEMAN

UPPER LAMBOURNE

Upper Lambourne is a market town in Berkshire; the surrounding downs are ideal for training racehorses; consequently many trainers have had their stables in this area. The poet is not thinking of one individual trainer, but of a typical one.

l. 9. **Carrara:** a type of marble that is quarried at a town in Italy of this name.

l. 20. **sarsen stone:** A type of sandstone found scattered on the chalk downs of Berkshire and Wiltshire. Most of the stones at Stonehenge are of this type.

YOUTH AND AGE ON BEAULIEU RIVER, HANTS

l. 1. **Beaulieu water:** a short wide river flowing into the Solent.

l. 10. **sharpie:** a long, sharp, flat-bottomed fishing boat.

VERSES TURNED IN AID OF ST. KATHERINE'S, CHISELHAMPTON

This little white church, on the edge of a small park, was built in 1763 in the classical style. Inside it the box pews, still in position, and the wooden altar-piece and tablets and candles make up an unspoiled Georgian interior.

l. 23. **pre-Tractarian:** belonging to a period before 1833-41, the years when the Tractarians, or members of the Oxford Movement, were publishing *Tracts for the Times*, which advocated more ritual in the Anglican service.

l. 26. **viol:** In the seventeenth and eighteenth centuries the music in church was usually provided by village instrumentalists who sat in the minstrel's gallery. They played old-fashioned instruments such as a viol (a six-stringed instrument) and serpent (a wooden wind-instrument with several bends). As Hardy's novels show, this music survived in many country churches till late in the nineteenth century.

l. 27. **Ken ... Tallis:** The well-known hymn 'Glory to Thee, my God, this night' has words by Bishop Ken (1637-1711) and music by Thomas Tallis (1505-85).

CHURCH OF ENGLAND THOUGHTS

Immediately west of the main bridge over the River Cherwell is one of Oxford's most beautiful buildings, the medieval tower of Magdalen College. On the opposite side of the High Street is the Botanic Garden.

l. 9. **Linnaean:** Linnaeus (1707) was a Swedish botanist whose method of classifying the names of plants is an essential foundation of modern biology.

l. 21. **chines:** literally, deep narrow ravines; presumably paths between tall bushes grown for their botanical interest.

l. 24. **churches:** As he listens, in the Botanic Garden, to the actual bells of Magdalen Tower, they mingle in his imagination with the remembered sounds of Church of England bells heard elsewhere.

l. 33. **sallies:** the woolly grips at the end of the bell-ropes.

CHRISTMAS

l. 2. **Tortoise stove:** This type of stove is still found in country churches. It burns coke; it is a round cast-iron stove about four feet high, and it has a tortoise on its top lid with the words 'slow but sure' inscribed round it.

l. 6. The colours of the stained-glass windows range from a purplish red to a vivid green. The names of these two colours attract Betjeman because they sound as though they are names of places.

THE VILLAGE INN

This poem satirises the advertisements published by brewers, and the false interest in the past professed by their architects and their Public Relations Officers. Betjeman is heavily ironical in lines such as 10–11 and 17–19. He particularly attacks the idea that the modern or modernised public house combines the beauty of an old building with an up-to-date emphasis on hygiene and health.

l. 4. **Hodge:** a traditional name for a farm labourer.

GREENAWAY

Greenaway is a shingle beach on the north coast of Cornwall, near Polzeath. It has particularly large waves at high tide.

l. 11. **bladderwrack:** seaweed which contains air-bladders.

l. 20. **cowries:** small shells.

HERTFORDSHIRE

l. 4. **syndicated shoots:** His father and a few friends or business acquaintances would combine to buy the right to shoot over a certain estate.

l. 7. **Lionel Edwards:** an artist, press illustrator and writer on sporting subjects. He was born in 1926.

DEATH IN LEAMINGTON

Leamington is chosen as typical of the spas that attracted large numbers of retired people from the upper classes, especially in the reigns of Victoria and Edward VII.

l. 10. This echoes Hood's poem about Ruth:

> *She stood breast high amid the corn,*
> *Clasp'd by the golden light of morn.*

Betjeman invites us to feel the tragedy of this old woman's death. She has presumably led a lonelier and lonelier life each year, and found it harder to keep up her former standards of living as prices rose — for the stucco is peeling off the front of the house. The Nurse is briskly competent and completely callous.

Betjeman achieves his effect by understatement, and by using a metre as out-of-date as the dead woman. It seems odd that Kenneth Allott should think this poem worth including in his *Contemporary Verse*, yet should say: *It represents the earlier, more facetious Betjeman and is relegated by Mr. Sparrow — who calls it, very happily, the poet's 'Innisfree' — to the poet's juvenilia.*

W. H. AUDEN

MISSING

John Lehmann has said that Auden's early poems imagine — *A world which seems to be in the throes of a strange guerilla campaign with secret conspiracies on all sides; dangerous frontiers to unknown countries which have to be crossed or not crossed; doom and catastrophe; the countryside is generally mountainous and apt to be filled with industrial ruins.*

If we do not look for any realistic or geographic consistency in the details, we are more likely to appreciate the force of these poems, which express the bewilderment of a young intelligent poet in the 1930's. Often Auden mixes the austere fells of the Lake District with the smokeless chimneys, damaged bridges, rotting wharves, and choked canals of the Midlands during the depression; but in this poem the second element is there only as a background from which the summer visitors escape.

This poem combines two themes that Auden was fond of during the thirties. There is the vague, melodramatic note of menace, of some imminent catastrophe. There is also the figure of the isolated Wanderer, the lonely leader (often an airman or a mountaineer or even a hawk) who looks down from a great height on the muddle below. He is divided from his followers by his intellectual superiority and by a certain stand-offish arrogance.

l. 1. **scars:** steep rocky sides of mountains in Northern England.

l. 7. **fell:** a ridge on the hills of Northern England.

l. 38. **Cape Wrath:** in the extreme north of Scotland.

FISH IN THE UNRUFFLED LAKES

In the first stanza Auden idealises animals and birds as more beautiful and perfect than humans and leading more complete lives. In the second stanza he says that we (humans as distinct from animals) allow our lives to be spoilt by self-consciousness, by a sense of guilt, and by worrying too much about time. In the third stanza he praises his beloved for having combined, at least on one occasion, the virtues of animals and humans. Many critics have pointed out the great emphasis which Auden attaches in his poetry to the word *love* (l. 27), its meaning, even in this early poem, is always wider than its erotic sense, and in his later poems the psycho-analytical conception of love is gradually extended until it seeks to unite the teachings of Christianity and psycho-analysis.

REFUGEE BLUES

The deliberately monotonous rhythm not only imitates jazz blues, it also suggests the weariness of a refugee speaking. He pretends to be flippant in order to stifle his bitter anger at the hardheartedness of everyone who ignores the needs of refugees. MacNeice makes similar use of jazz rhythms in *Bagpipe Music*.

BIRTHDAY POEM
(*To Christopher Isherwood*)

Christopher Isherwood became friends with Auden in 1914 when both were sent to the same preparatory school: Isherwood was ten and Auden was seven. Although they went to different schools and universities later, they collaborated in writing two verse plays in the 1930's and emigrated to America together. As a young man Isherwood wrote promising novels, but he has written less frequently and less successfully since going to America.

ll. 1–24. Auden writes a skilful piece of poetic journalism about how the British went on holiday in 1935; for the moment he is writing about the present.

ll. 25–40. He looks back to a holiday they spent on the Isle of Wight in 1926; Auden was nineteen and they were *half-boys* (l. 27).

Tennyson (l. 26) wrote his best poetry before he left his native Lincolnshire. In 1853 he went to live on the Isle of Wight; the poems that he wrote from this point onward appealed strongly to the Victorians but today they seem less genuine and moving than his earlier writing.

ll. 41–56. refer to Auden's visit to the Baltic in 1931 — the *now* of l. 41 could be misleading. They are shy of conventional society.

These lines are an interesting early expression of Auden's hope that love (l. 42) may regenerate society even to the point of curing anti-semitism (l. 47).

ll. 57–96. return to the present, i.e. to 1935. They give a satirical description of the world not yet recovered from the great economic slump and already blundering towards the second world war. Already the radios blare forth the propaganda of Hitler and others (ll. 59–60). Auden urges Isherwood to write in such a way as to 'make action urgent and its nature clear' and not to fall into the mood of the Russian upper classes before 1917, sitting in elegant and cultured despair around their *stoves* (l. 64); Auden is thinking of how they seemed resigned to defeat in the plays of Chekhov.

l. 68. **Weeping Cross:** In the Middle Ages it was a common practice to raise crosses at crossroads so that penitents could bewail their sins there.

1st September 1939

Hitler invaded Poland on this day, and so began the second world war. Auden hears the news in the *neutral air* of New York, for the U.S.A. did not enter the war until December 1941. His conversational style represents the mood of resignation of those who now found themselves face to face with the disaster they had expected. The verse form and the style are copied from Yeats's 'Easter 1916'; both poems are grave, but undramatic, comments on political events.

l. 1. **dives:** drinking dens in cellars; they had been illegal during Prohibition.

l. 2. **Fifty-second Street:** an unsavoury street of warehouses and tenements.

l. 8. **darkened:** both by the black-out and by the spiritual darkness of war.

ll. 14–15. **Luther:** Martin Luther (1483–1546) led the reformation in Germany. His narrow patriotism may have helped to distort the 'culture' of the Germans, making them aggressive and over-confident.

l. 16. **Linz.** A town in Austria. Hitler was born near there.

l. 17. **imago:** We imagine an ideal god or hero, and base our notion of this god or hero on our own father or mother. We subconsciously admire what approaches this ideal.

l. 18. **A psychopathic God:** Hitler, or Hitler's idea of good.

l. 23. **Thucydides:** The Greek historian whose book describes convincingly the futility of the war between Sparta and Athens.

l. 43. **euphoric:** of well-being.

l. 59. **Nijinsky:** A famous Russian ballet dancer (1890–1950).

l. 60. **Diaghilev:** (1872–1929) A Russian producer, who staged beautiful ballets and operas in London, Paris and America.

l. 96. **Eros:** originally the god of love, Cupid; but Auden uses the term for a selfish type of love.

When this poem was first published in *Another Time* in 1940 it contained an extra stanza:

> *All I have is a voice*
> *To undo the folded lie;*
> *The romantic lie in the brain*
> *Of the sensual man-in-the-street*
> *And the lie of Authority*
> *Whose buildings grope the sky:*
> *There is no such thing as the state*
> *And no-one exists alone;*
> *Hunger allows no choice*
> *To the citizen or the police;*
> *We must love one another or die.*

It is interesting as showing Auden's attitude and ideas moving closer to Christianity. Joseph Warren Beach, in *The Making of the Auden Canon*, accuses Auden of omitting this stanza because *the statement is not made here in specifically and unmistakable religious terms.* Monroe K. Spears is surely right in *The Poetry of W. H. Auden* when he dismisses Beach's argument and says that Auden omitted the stanza on aesthetic grounds — that it is too 'explicit and facile'.

THE UNKNOWN CITIZEN

Auden satirises bureaucratic society in which the importance of the individual is minimised.

The rhythm resembles the sprung rhythm of Gerard Manley Hopkins. Each line has four accented syllables, but the number of unstressed syllables in each foot varies.

THE MANAGERS

The poem contrasts our modern overworked rulers with those who ruled our ancestors in *the bad old days.* Auden pictures our modern rulers as lacking glamour; their only pleasure is a selfish love of power.

Auden is vague about when the *bad old days* came to an end; during them a ruler could be obviously and selfishly richer than his subjects, having as many wives or mistresses or horses or palaces as he liked. But today *Honours are not so physical or jolly*; consequently in democratic countries the rulers are exposed to the full glare of publicity, and are forced to live abstemious and respectable lives.

Auden begins with a kind of irony. As a Christian he is slightly amused by the crude selfishness of past rulers, though he cannot really approve of them. He goes on to suggest that our present-day rulers, gaining nothing from being in office except the pleasure of exercising power, may be denying the deeper Christian purposes of life in a more subtle and serious way than the old type of ruler ever did. He condemns as forgetful of God the modern overworked President or Prime Minister, whose signature might cause far greater slaughter than the animal greed of Attila or Jenghiz Khan ever did.

l. 12. **deck**: American for a pack of cards.

l. 17. **The Tragic Hero**: Aristotle described him as a great, fundamentally good man who comes to a disastrous end through one fault. Hamlet, who comes to his doom through procrastination, or Othello, who is ruined by jealousy, or the hero of almost any tragedy by Shakespeare or the Greek tragedians, illustrates Aristotle's idea.

　　the Platonic Saint: Plato imagined a ruling class who would be educated to be virtuous.

ll. 18–21. Can anyone imagine a modern painter painting today's Prime Minister naked and surrounded by cherubs, as Rubens and other painters depicted the rulers of their day?

EMBASSY

As in 'The Managers', Auden emphasises how much depends on the routine decisions of the rulers.

THE SHIELD OF ACHILLES

In the *Iliad* Achilles sulked in his tent because he had been slighted by the Greek leaders. His friend Patroclus borrowed his armour, thinking that the Trojans would take him for Achilles and run away. But Hector killed Patroclus and took away his borrowed armour. Achilles blamed himself bitterly for having caused his friend's death.

His mother, Thetis, a goddess, appeared to him and promised to ask Hephaestos (or Vulcan, the blacksmith of the gods, the lame husband of Venus) to make new armour for him.

In Book XVIII of the *Iliad* Thetis looks over Hephaestos' shoulder at the shield he has made. At different places on the shield the god had decorated it with designs of happy scenes, such as marriages and harvestings, but at other places he had represented horrific scenes of battles or lions attacking cattle: in other words Homer's divine blacksmith places in realistic juxtaposition the beauty and horror of life.

Auden does not correct Homer; he merely writes variations on Homer's theme, and gives us a total view of evil in all ages from Homer's day till now. In his poem Thetis looks over Hephaestos' shoulder expecting to see conventional representations of happiness; instead she sees a timeless representation of the evil of the ages, in which a radio propagandist defends the wrong, Pontius Pilate is a bored bureaucrat putting up barbed wire round Christ's cross, and a typical juvenile delinquent throws a stone at a bird. The far-seeing Hephaestos has created a terrible picture of man's inhumanity to man throughout the ages.

IN PRAISE OF LIMESTONE

This poem is an interesting metrical experiment. The lines generally speaking have thirteen and eleven syllables alternately; when a word ends with a vowel and the next word begins with a vowel or an *h*, elision is intended.

When he is in America, Auden is homesick for the limestone hills of northern England, for

> *The limestone moors that stretch from* Brough
> *To* Hexham *and the* Roman Wall.

In this poem he expresses his homesickness for the Appennines, the limestone hills of Italy, which remind him of the Pennines. (Many of his later poems study landscapes as causes or symbols of men's psychological tendencies.) As he gazes at the limestone hills, and contrasts them with the plains and river valleys, they begin to stand for conflicting human impulses, such as man's desire to settle down in a familiar place and his wanderlust.

l. 22. **gennels**: a northern dialect word; literally, a narrow lane or entry between houses or gardens.

ll. 42–54. The 'best and worst' of mankind seek other types of soil or landscape, such as granite or clay and gravel.

l. 55. **slamming the door**: Goebbels, Hitler's minister for propaganda, said: 'If we are defeated, we shall slam the door of history behind us'.

ll. 55–56. The 'really reckless' are attracted by the ocean.

ll. 60–93. The people whom Auden resembles, and whose faults he admits as well as praising their humanity and individuality, are attracted to the landscapes formed by the limestone hills.

l. 86. **modifications of matter**: statues.

R. S. THOMAS

WELSH LANDSCAPE

ll. 1–3. As he looks at the sky at sunset it seems stained with the blood of Welshmen who died resisting Roman, Saxon, Norman and English invaders. A. E. Housman writes similarly in 'The Welsh Marches':

> *The vanquished eve, as night prevails,*
> *Bleeds upon the road to Wales.*

A WELSH TESTAMENT

l. 10. **Glyn Dwr**: Owen Glendower (to anglicise his name) rebelled against Henry IV in 1400 and proclaimed himself the last independent Prince of Wales. For some years he held various

parts of Wales against the English king and allied with various
rebels such as Hotspur, as Shakespeare shows in *Henry IV, pt. I*.
Glendower even set up a Welsh Parliament at Machynlleth.
When he died in 1416 the rebellion collapsed, but in modern
times the Welsh have come to regard him as a national hero.
Thomas is, firstly, insisting that to him as a priest the characters
of his parishioners are all important. But he is also pleading for
an economic policy that will help the hill farmer to conquer his
geographic problems, and the hard conditions of life that blunt
his mind and kill his spirit. It should be stressed that six Welsh
counties have smaller populations than they had 100 years ago.

THE POACHER

l. 13. **familiar:** close friend.

THE DARK WELL

l. 5. **Prytherch:** Thomas's name for the typical hill-farmer who
works hard on his small, infertile holding. Thomas has written
several poems about this man.

NINETIETH BIRTHDAY

ll. 12–13. **the far sea's signal:** As he climbs higher up the hilly
track, Thomas sees the sunlight glinting on the sea far below.

l. 18. **the lost village:** She thinks that the village, which she lives a
long way from, is just as it was when she was young. But it is
changed out of recognition; the village she thinks of no longer
exists.

THE MUSICIAN

l. 1. **Kreisler:** a famous violinist. He was born in Vienna in 1875
and died in the U.S.A. in 1962.

l. 10. **neurosis:** a nervous derangement, which might cause one's
fingers to twitch.

THE VILLAGE

ll. 9–13. So little happens in this village (obviously Manafon in
Montgomeryshire) that for a black dog to crack fleas is an event,
breaking the monotony of the afternoon. But the girl, as a
representative of the village people — in their light and shade,
and their joys and sorrows — is more important than any event.

ll. 14–17. This village is the centre of a rural world whose living
people mean as much to the poet as Plato's imaginary world
meant to the philosopher. To Thomas, the life of his parishioners

assumes a universal importance, because his poetry springs from his attempt as a parish priest to understand their life and personalities.

THE VIEW FROM THE WINDOW

It thinks of the natural scene as a painting painted by God.

A BLACKBIRD SINGING

l. 1. **it seems wrong:** Thomas begins with a feeling he is soon to disown: he wishes that light and dark, good and evil were separated more distinctly, instead of being mixed as they are when so black a bird sings so beautiful a song.

ll. 5–6. Just as alchemy turns a common metal to gold, so the bright orange of the blackbird's bill gives him a golden song, and also the magic of life as it really is turns light and dark, good and evil, into a more complex unity than Thomas was prepared to accept at first.

ll. 11–16. Thomas thinks of the blackbird as remembering instinctively and subconsciously all that his ancestors have experienced. But it remains a real bird in a way that Keats's nightingale does not.

What biologists have taught about evolution and what psychologists have taught about heredity have helped build up Thomas's conception of how the blackbird, like the poet, combines the communal memory of one's race with a personal originality of expression.

This is so intense a poem that one is surprised to be shown, after reading it, that it is unrhymed. Each line has a free rhythm with four stressed syllables.

DYLAN THOMAS

THE FORCE THAT THROUGH THE GREEN FUSE

There are several deliberate similarities between the five stanzas. The first four begin with *The*, have a strong caesura (or pause) in the middle of the second line, and have the same five words at the beginning of the fourth line. The last lines of all the stanzas except the first begin with *How*.

ll. 1–5. Thomas thinks of himself as part of the same explosive force that energises or creates everything in Nature. It is a force that brings both life and death, creation and destruction; it blasts as well as fusing.

l. 2. **green age:** youth.

l. 4. **crooked** combines the various meanings of the word — old, deformed, criminal.

    dumb: It means both inarticulate and foolish.

    to tell: by writing poetry.

l. 5. Old men and adolescents are thought of as equally unsuccessful in love.

ll. 6-10. Water running through rocks resembles blood flowing through veins, and also a vein or ore running through rocks.

l. 13. **shroud sail:** a possible reference to the legend of Theseus. Theseus, son of the ruler of Athens, sailed to Crete as one of the seven youths and seven maidens who went every ninth year to Crete as tribute, and were normally killed by the Minotaur. The ship that took them to their doom always used a black sail. Theseus promised his father, Aegeus, that if he survived his ordeal in Crete, he would change the sail to a white one; but he forgot to do this, and when his father saw the ship in the distance returning with a black sail, he threw himself to his death from the high rock of the Acropolis.

l. 14. **the hanging man:** both the embryo curled up in the womb, and the executed criminal.

l. 15. **hangman's lime:** in which the corpses of criminals were buried after their hanging.

l. 16. **leech:** to suck, as a leech does.

l. 18. **her:** the mother's. Thomas is obsessed with the idea of birth.

l. 22. **sheet:** It is simultaneously the shroud or winding-sheet that the coffin-worm eats, the bed-sheet covering the phallus, and the sheet of paper on which the poet's finger writes.

AND DEATH SHALL HAVE NO DOMINION

This was the first of Thomas's poems to be published — in 1933 — and it shows that he began, as he ended, as a lyricist. Like an inspired preacher, Thomas is conducting a service for all the dead on the certainty of their resurrection.

The repeated first line is an adaptation of St. Paul, Romans vi. 9: *Death hath no more dominion.*

ll. 1-9. The dead — their bones picked clean — will be re-created on Judgement Day. They will be joined to the wind and stars in a united Creation.

l. 3. A typical transposition of the man in the moon and the west wind.

l. 6. Even if they were mad when they died, they will be sane when they rise again.

ll. 13-18. Martyrs will rise again, even if they lost faith when they were tortured.

l. 16. **unicorn:** here thought of as the most savage of beasts.

ll. 17-18. Thomas may be remembering Revelation xx. 13: *And the sea gave up the dead which were in it.* He often associates the sea with death; for instance, in *Under Milk Wood — the lights of the lamps in the windows call back the day and the dead that have run away to sea.*

l. 25. **hammer**: force their way upward through the surface of the soil and the *daisies* whom the dead are colloquially said to be *pushing up.*

THE HAND THAT SIGNED THE PAPER

This poem is not propaganda, for the rheumaticky hand that did so much harm with one signature might as well have been that of a constitutional king as of a dictator. Here Thomas is emphasising the impersonality of modern power-politics.

l. 2. So efficient a tyranny taxed even life itself.

l. 4. **These five kings**: his five fingers.

l. 6. The finger-joints have arthritis as well as writer's cramp.

l. 7. The tyrant becomes benign — at least temporarily.

l. 8. But he finds a way of reducing free speech.

l. 15. **rules**: limits, restricts.

POEM IN OCTOBER

ll. 1–10. He describes how he leaves Laugharne. It is early morning. The scene is so holy that the water seems to be praying and the herons seems to be priests for they stand on the shore, surrounded by kitty-wakes and oyster-catchers, and adopt attitudes like that of a priest blessing his parishioners. In such a small country town near the sea rooks and seagulls will be flying together.

ll. 11–20. The poet walks through a scene that is a beautiful confusion of actuality and memory, of country and sea, of the sun and rain of a sunshine shower.

ll. 21–30. Suddenly the larks sing as though it were spring and the October sun shines as though it were summer, whereas up till now he had *wandered and listened to the rain.*

ll. 31–40. Just as his eye sees sunshine and rain at once, so his mind's eye sees past and present scenes at once.

ll. 41–50. He turns away from looking at Laugharne in the October sun to think of wonderful summer mornings when he was a child at Swansea or Fern Hill.

l. 48. **parables**: the sunlight taught him about God's goodness, just as parables do.

l. 50. **green chapels**: woods.

l. 52. As *his* tears burned *my* cheeks, the *man* of thirty, and the *boy* he remembers, became one. Past and present, Swansea and Laugharne, are united.

l. 56. **summertime of the dead**: the boy's past summers, when his aunt (Anne Jones) and others who were then dear to him were still living

ll. 61–70. It repeats phrases of the first, fourth, and sixth stanzas.

l. 62. **the weather turned round**: his thoughts return to the actual present.

l. 63. **The long dead child**: the child that he once was.

ll. 65–70. He is aware simultaneously of the summer noon of his childhood that he remembers and of the red leaves of October present in the town below.

ll. 68–70. May he write equally well on his hill above Laugharne in a year's time!

FERN HILL

Fern Hill was a farm near Llanbri, between Carmarthen and Llanstephan; it was the home of the poet's aunt, Anne Jones, whose death is mourned in an early poem — *After the Funeral*. The poem shows that Dylan Thomas remembers how he enjoyed holidays spent there away from Swansea, and now idealises the excitement and innocence of childhood in the way that Vaughan, Rousseau and Wordsworth did.

Thomas is trying to communicate the exhilaration which he felt as a child, and which gives such vitality and freshness to the short stories about childhood that he called *Portrait of the Artist as a Young Dog*. To do this his poetry uses language in a very original and eloquent way, and the reader has to co-operate by taking this sparkling torrent of words in the spirit in which it is written and not to expect individual words to have the exact meaning or grammatical construction that they normally have. There is much repetition: he is *easy under the* apple *boughs* and *prince of the* apple *towns*. In fact, *green* is repeated in each stanza. There are startling similes such as *fire green as grass*.

There are many transferred epithets such as:

> spellbound horses *walking warm*
> *Out of the* whinnying *green* stable.

There are repeated unsystematic references to the buildings of the farm where Dylan is living or staying.

The metaphors are arresting in various ways. When he 'rode to sleep' the verb reminds us how the child, falling asleep after an exciting day, continues in sleep the sensations and movements of the unforgettable day. Similarly in 'A Visit to Grandpa's' the boy has *a dream full of whips and lariats as long as serpents, and runaway coaches on mountain passes, and wide windy gallops over cactus fields*. The metaphor *it was Adam and maiden* gains its effect by compression; we sense that the boy's life had the freshness and innocence that life had in the Garden of Eden when Adam first met the virgin Eve. The poem also contains continual exaggeration as when the hay fields were *high as the house*. But these hyperboles show us how things seemed to a child, just as phrases such as *all the moon long* show how a child measures time. The poem exalts childhood for the child was *honoured, lordly* and *famous*.

Most of the poem is capable of paraphrase; for instance, l. 6 means: 'I felt as important and honoured as a prince when I played among the farm wagons or among the apple trees which surrounded me like buildings of a town'. Or ll. 17 and 18 mean: 'The sound of the streams over the pebbles called me to worship Nature just as the church bells on the sabbath call Christians to worship'. But to paraphrase such lines is to destroy Thomas's musical effects and the strong emotional responses of his evocative images.

The first two stanzas (ll. 1–18) describe the boy's impressions of innocent but self-centred happiness on one wonderful day. In ll. 23–24 he goes to sleep and dreams that the owls and nightjars whisk the farm away. In ll. 28–29 it comes back at dawn as the boy wakes up and it looks wet with dew as though it has been out all night. The farm comes to life again as though the miracle of The Creation is being repeated. In l. 37 Dylan is *honoured* not merely among wagons but *among foxes and pheasants*: he has been accepted as part of Nature. But the stanza ends with the first suggestion that this childhood happiness cannot last, and Time, in the last stanza, leads him to the loft to sleep again. When he wakes on this second morning (l. 51) the swallows, the symbols of his innocence, will have flown away, and the land will be childless because his childhood is over.

THE HUNCHBACK IN THE PARK

It is noticeable that when Thomas wrote poetry about childhood, it had greater clarity and more compassion. In this poem his memory returns to Cwmdonkin Park in Swansea, where he loved to play as a boy.

This poem creates three worlds, the worlds of the hunchback and the teasing boys, who have no understanding of one another, and the third world of the poet, who now understands both the others.

Just as the boys 'made' tigers (l. 28) in their daydreams, so the hunchback 'made' a *woman figure without fault in his daydreams*. The boys think of themselves as young dogs, so they think of the hunchback as an old dog (l. 25).

l. 4. **lock**: the lock, acting like one in a canal, lets the water and trees enter when the public enters the park in the morning, and lets them out together at night.

IN MY CRAFT OR SULLEN ART

l. 1. **sullen (art)**: He uses the word to stress how lonely and unsociable the poet must be as he works.

l. 6. **singing light**: the light that inspires him to write poetry.

l. 8. **(not for) the strut and trade of charms**: He dismisses the rhetorical and magical qualities of others' poetry.

l. 10. He writes poetry for ordinary men, who pay him very small wages.

ll. 11–12. He does not write for proud business men, administrators and politicians, who are quite indifferent to the moon and to the imagination or sense of beauty that it symbolises.

A REFUSAL TO MOURN THE DEATH, BY FIRE, OF A CHILD IN LONDON

The first sentence lasts for 13 lines and ends appropriately with the word *death*. The main verb, *shall*, does not occur till l. 10. Thomas says that he will not mourn the child's death until the darkness that makes mankind (and so fathers bird, beast, and flower) brings the world — and even the tumbling sea — to an end. Since darkness precedes birth, it is said to be a maker and a father.

l. 3. **humbling:** Darkness (whether death or sleep or the state of being unborn) makes us all equally powerless.

ll. 7–13. At his death the atoms that compose the poet's body will be turned into water and corn; the use of metaphors from religion suggests that this will be a holy process. On the Last Day Thomas, as the representative of mankind, must return to the seed and water from which he came and to which the child has returned before him.

l. 15. **grave:** a pun.

l. 20. **long friends:** grains of London's earth, friends of long standing.

l. 24. The meaning is complex: after we have been shocked by one death in our lives, no other is so devastating: also, after the death of the body there is no death of the soul. It is unlikely to mean 'when you are dead, that's the end', because there is a consistent belief in a resurrection throughout Thomas's poetry.

DO NOT GO GENTLE INTO THAT GOOD NIGHT

A villanelle is a poem normally in five tercets and a quatrain. It uses only two rhymes, which form a strict sequence, and the first and third lines are repeated in an elaborate pattern. It is paradoxical that Thomas should choose so formal and artificial a structure, usually associated with light verse and Austin Dobson, for this very personal poem on his father's illness in old age.

l. 1. **good night:** It combines the ideas of saying farewell, of God be with you, and of death as a natural end to life.

ll. 1–3. The two rhyming words, *night* and *light*, stand for death and life. Thomas urges his father not to accept death tamely. *Rage* is an echo of several of Yeats's poems about old age.

ll. 4–6. Philosophers accept death as a natural, inevitable end.

ll. 7-9. Puritans are not ready for death, because they at last realise they have missed opportunities to lead a full life.

ll. 10-12. Hedonists cannot accept death stoically.

ll. 13-14. Men who are *grave*, wise in a serious way, regret the approach of death because they see clearly how much old men might have achieved.

l. 14. **gay**: a deliberate echo of Yeats's 'Lapis Lazuli'.

PHILIP LARKIN

I REMEMBER, I REMEMBER

We are intended to recall the rather sentimental poem, *Past and Present*, by Thomas Hood, which is No. 224 in Palgrave's *Golden Treasury*. It begins:

> *I remember, I remember*
> *The house where I was born,*
> *The little window where the sun*
> *Came peeping in at morn;*
> *He never came a wink too soon*
> *Nor brought too long a day.*
> *But now, I often wish the night*
> *Had borne my breath away.*

Hood thinks of childhood as happy and innocent; the roses were red and white, robins built nests in the lilac, and when he used to swing, he thought the tops of the fir trees reached up to the sky. Actually, the parts of the poem that deal directly with childhood are more successful than Hood's maudlin contrast between the happiness of being a child and the misery of being an adult.

Larkin sets out to tell the truth about his own childhood, and not to claim, as Hood or Rousseau or Wordsworth or Dylan Thomas did, that:

> *All the sun long it was running, it was lovely, the hay*
> *Fields high as the house. . . . .*
> *It was Adam and maiden.*

ll. 17-36. are a satirical dig at autobiographical novels that give dramatic accounts of the author's childhood and adolescence.

CHURCH GOING

There is a punning ambiguity in the title; the poem is about Larkin going into a church and also about the Church as an institution disintegrating.

ll. 1-2. He is shy about entering a church and waits till there is nothing unusual going on before he does so.

ll. 21–52. He speculates on what churches would look like if Christianity lost its believers, and what superstitious motives would still lead women to visit them after dark. He wonders who will be the last, if this happens, to visit the building while it is still whole; will it be an expert on church architecture or a connoiseur of ritual, or will it be someone like himself who values it because it preserves or commemorates so much of the past?

l. 25. **pyx:** a vessel in which consecrated bread is kept.

l. 30. **simples:** herbs used as medicine.

l. 41. **rood-loft:** singing gallery on the top of the rood screen, at the west end of the church.

ll. 52–63. He moves on to express deeper feelings of respect for what churches seem to him, and of regret that their future is so uncertain.

THE WHITSUN WEDDINGS

ll. 1–10. He is obviously leaving Hull, a fishing port separated from Lincolnshire by the Humber. With his usual dependable sense of style, Larkin transmutes realistic details of the views from a train window to elegant poetry.

ll. 21–80. The various bridal couples, waving goodbye to friends and dodging fresh showers of confetti as they board the train, are unreflective; but the observant bachelor poet, becoming involved in their experience, understands their feelings which they are too preoccupied to do.

l. 80. **rain:** It is welcomed here as a traditional symbol of fertility. Coming after drought, it guarantees the renewal of life.

AT GRASS

C. B. Cox and A. E. Dyson praise this poem in *Modern Poetry : Studies in Practical Criticism.* They point out that *The old racehorses are first seen lost in shadow. We are made to feel the pathos of the swift passing of time, and of the brevity of triumph. Words like 'cold' and 'distresses' make the horses seem pathetic in their retirement.*

The second stanza expresses surprise that 'two dozen distances', twenty-four victories by a neck or a short head, could make them *fabulous* as the horses that won the *classics.*

Whereas Yeats's swan or Eliot's river is a symbol, Larkin's horses are merely horses. Larkin ends with the idea that there is some joy in resignation and in being free from the need to race and compete, but possibly as the horses submit to the boy who comes with a bridle at the end of the poem, we are intended to feel that death is imminent.

In his introduction to *The New Poetry* Alvarez accuses poets since Eliot of lacking 'seriousness', and complains that the fault of this poem is *gentility*:

Larkin's poem, elegant and unpretentious and rather beautiful in its gentle way, is a nostalgic recreation of the Platonic (or New Yorker) idea of the English scene, part pastoral, part sporting. His horses are *social* creatures of fashionable race meetings and high style; emotionally, they belong to the R.S.P.C.A.

Alvarez goes on to prefer Ted Hughes's 'A Dream of Horses' because it has more urgency; but this is a futile type of criticism which, instead of evaluating the poem, blames it for not being another type of poem on another topic. Larkin's artistic triumph is to adopt a tone and style appropriate to his actual topic.

l. 13. **silks**: coloured blouses worn by jockeys.

LINES ON A YOUNG LADY'S PHOTOGRAPH ALBUM

l. 8. **sweet girl-graduate**: This is a semi-humorous echo of l. 142 of Tennyson's *The Princess* — *Sweet girl-graduates in their golden hair*.

l. 20. **Hall's Distemper boards**: Boards advertising Hall's distemper are often seen in the middle of fields beside railway lines.

l. 35. **yowl**: howl, yell.

WEDDING WIND

ll. 1–10. The wind, banging the stable door, is an interruption of the happiness of the speaker's wedding night.

ll. 10–16. The wind is no longer an interruption of her happiness, but a symbol or manifestation of it.

ll. 17–20. Her joy holds her actions together just as a thread holds beads together. Her happiness, of which the wind is a symbol, is almost too great to bear; she wonders whether she will ever be allowed to return to a humdrum, unemotional life symbolised by *sleep*.

ll. 20–23. Her husband and she herself, enjoying endless happiness, are compared to cattle drinking the water of a lake that never will dry up.

TOADS

l. 10. **lispers**: those who adopt affected voices to gain money.

l. 11. **losels**: ne'er-do-wells.

loblolly-men: surgeon's attendants (nautical slang). They earn their living by doing unpleasant jobs for other people.

l. 24. Prospero in *The Tempest* (IV. 1. ll. 156–8) says of the human race:

> *We are such stuff*
> *As dreams are made on; and our little life*
> *Is rounded with a sleep.*

Prospero regards our everyday, matter-of-fact life as an illusory dream, and asserts that even reality is unreal. Larkin deliberately translates Prospero's statement into something much more prosaic — he labels only our daydreams as 'the stuff that dreams are made on'.

l. 27. **hunkers**: the backs of one's thighs.

ll. 33–34. One 'toad' is work; 'the other' toad is the impetus within him that drives him to work.

AN ARUNDEL TOMB

Larkin is thinking of a tomb of a member of the Arundel family that is in Chichester Cathedral.

l. 3. **proper habits**: These technical terms in heraldry mean that their dress was in natural, not conventional, colours.

l. 7. **pre-baroque**: The tomb was built before the baroque style of architecture and sculpture — which used a lot of fantastic ornamentation — became popular in the seventeenth century.

ll. 21–24. The general state of the tomb, and the way the cathedral was affected by the Civil War and other religious changes (i.e. *its air*) was such that time subtly and gradually (*soundlessly*) damaged it, taking the newness and clarity off the inscription. Enclosures and the agricultural revolution removed, or changed the attitudes of, the old type of tenant of the Arundel family (whose castle and lands passed to the Duke of Norfolk by marriage in 1580). Visitors began to look at the tomb without reading it because they no longer understood Latin.

ll. 27–29. The life of Nature seems unorganised. Birdcalls seem distributed over the cathedral's burial-ground as haphazardly as the bones — now disarranged by later burials. The birdcalls are *bright* in the sense of cheerful, and because they are associated with daylight and life above the ground.

l. 33. **unarmorial**: The present age is not interested in heraldry and in coats of arms.

l. 34. **smoke**: Even cathedral cities now have smoke from houses and factories suspended in the air above them.

l. 40. **blazon**: a means of recording their virtues by adding details to their coats of arms.

A DREAM OF HORSES

The speaker is a groom to the horses of a vaguely oriental ruler who lived in a palace near a desert; presumably these are past events.

Ll. 1-3 and ll. 21-24 are matter-of-fact and ordinary; but ll. 4-20 use violent language in order to suggest a nightmare. The grooms dream that wild horses from the desert attack the palace stables at night, while their own tame horses try to kick their way out. The grooms are too amazed to *do* anything. But in the morning the desert sands remain *unprinted,* because the attackers were *dream* horses.

l. 7. **mice in our pockets:** This is Hughes's exaggerated way of saying that in the stable the mice and grooms slept so close together that the mice might just as well have been in their pockets.

l. 8. **avalanching:** falling as abruptly and noisily as an avalanche does.

l. 19. **dream:** In their nightmare they act as though in a daze.

ll. 21–24. The speaker and the other grooms wake up.

l. 24. **hag-sweat:** a sweat produced by witchcraft. The phrase is suggested by the word *hagridden*, meaning 'afflicted by nightmares, especially those sent by witches'.

l. 25. **quartered:** Hughes uses the word to combine two specially unpleasant forms of capital punishment. *Quartered* normally means *cut up into four*, as the bodies of traitors often were; here it also reminds us of the grisly punishment of tying the criminal's four limbs to four different horses, which are then whipped till they gallop off in four directions.

ll. 25–27. Half-awakened from his dreams, the speaker day-dreams about the future. This too will be dominated by horses. The general idea of doomsday's flames resembling horses may be suggested by the visions of the horsemen of the Apocalypse in Revelations vi and Zechariah vi, but there is no precise parallel between l. 26 and any detail in the Biblical descriptions of the Last Day.

THE JAGUAR

l. 6. **is:** resembles.

ll. 12–13. The jaguar's eyes pierce the onlookers — and also the darkness — as though they were electric drills; they are like a train of gunpowder with a short fuse, likely to explode suddenly.

l. 18. The fierceness of his stride is so intense that he has achieved a kind of freedom in reaching such an intensity of fierceness.

The half-rhymes are the sort that we associate with Cecil Day Lewis or Louis MacNeice; they derive from Owen's para-rhymes, but keep to far less rigorous rules than those did.

THE THOUGHT-FOX

He imagines a fox, and this fox in his thoughts becomes virtually real. It is also the thought that is the basis of the poem; it is an image of the process of poetic creation.

ll. 9–22. The running-on of the rhythm from one stanza to another suggests the wary movement of the fox.

l. 22. **the dark hole of the head:** the poet's brain.

l. 24. **the page is printed:** He has written his poem.

WIND

l. 1. The wind has been blowing so hard around the house that the house seems like a ship out at sea.

l. 6. **The hills had new places:** So violent a wind seemed to have moved even them.

l. 11. **brunt:** Hughes uses the familiar noun as an unfamiliar adjective.

A WOMAN UNCONSCIOUS

ll. 3–4. An atomic war would melt even Mother Earth.

ll. 5–7. **The quick . . . insect:** The real life active in the world would be burned out; all that the successive ages of man have achieved would be lost — and all leaves and insects would die too.

ll. 11–12. It may never happen.

ll. 17–24. The word that emphasises the contrast with what precedes it is *lesser*. The death of one (l. 22) is not a lesser death (l. 20) than that of all mankind. The fact that America and Russia may be planning to blow us all up, does not reduce the tragedy of one woman's illness and possible death.

AN OTTER

The structure of the poem produces several impressive contrasts. There is one between the otter living naturally (ll. 1–20) and the otter hiding under water from the hounds and huntsmen (ll. 21–28); there is another between the live otter (ll. 1–38) and the dead otter (ll. 39–40).

l. 7. **vermin-poles:** the gibbets on which gamekeepers used to hang the animals whom they classed as vermin and then killed.

l. 20. **walloping:** The word combines the idea of *galloping* with wandering.

THRUSHES

ll. 2–11. **steel . . . triggered . . . bullet . . . automatically:** The associations of these words with industry or warfare stress the ruthless efficiency of the thrushes.

ll. 17–20. Whatever activity a man chooses, whether he forces himself to be heroic on horseback or works conscientiously in an office, or executes a piece of carving in a slow, patient manner, 'his act worships itself' — i.e. he is self-consciously aware of his own technique or style in doing this; the thrush, on the other hand, instinctively and immediately catches a worm; it does not stop to think 'How wonderful my worm-stabbing technique is!' or 'I wonder whether I stab better with my back to the sun'.

ll. 20–24. Ordinary man — unlike geniuses (e.g. Mozart), thrushes and sharks — is often distracted from his main purpose. All distractions are like devils, but some make us happy and others make us unhappy. *Orgy, hosanna* and *weep* are verbs describing the hidden forces in man that distract him from his main purpose. There is a distinction between energies that are beleaguered with the complications of heaven and hell, and those which are not.

INDEX OF FIRST LINES